Biancastella

A Jewish Partisan in World War II

40°
ANNIVERSARIO
INSURREZIONE
E LIBERAZIONE

27-28
APRILE
1945

COMUNE DI CUNEO
COMITATO ANTIFASCISTA DI CUNEO

Biancastella

*A Jewish Partisan in
World War II*

Harry Burger
edited by Larry Borowsky

UNIVERSITY PRESS OF COLORADO

© 1997 by the University Press of Colorado

Published by the University Press of Colorado
P.O. Box 849
Niwot, Colorado 80544

Library of Congress Cataloging-in-Publication Data

Burger, Harry. 1924-
    Biancastella : a Jewish partisan in World War II /
    Harry Burger [with Larry Borowsky].
            p.   cm.
    Includes index.
    ISBN 0-87081-397-8 (alk. paper)
    1. Burger, Harry, 1924-   . 2. Jews—Austria—
Vienna—Biography. 3. Holocaust, Jewish (1939-1945)—
France—Personal narratives. 4. World War, 1939-1945—
Underground movements—Italy.
I. Borowsky, Larry, 1963-   . II. Title.
    DS135.A93B87—dc21
    [B]   96-52672
                                                   CIP

Contents

INTRODUCTION

During World War II I fought as a member of the Italian First Alpine Division, better known as the Partisans, a guerrilla outfit that formed shortly after the fall of Mussolini in 1943. For two years we battled the Nazis in the foothills of northwestern Italy. They had more men and much better equipment, but we were more determined and knew the terrain better than they. We held them at bay until the end of the war.

As a Partisan I went by the name *Biancastella*. I was not the only one to use a nom de guerre—almost everybody had one. But for me the change of identities was particularly significant. Unlike my comrades, I was not Italian; I was an Austrian Jew on the run from the Nazis. My comrades knew my true identity and accepted me as an equal. But we guerrillas needed to be able to disappear into the civilian population, and I would have stuck out like a sore thumb if I'd used my real name.

More than my name changed during the war. I had grown up in a well-to-do family; my father owned a very successful textile company, and I was being groomed to take over the family business. I was fourteen when the war began, twenty-one by the time it was over, and in those years the prospects for my future were forever altered. I became not the man I hoped to be but the man I had to be.

But one cannot choose the circumstances under which one comes of age.

▫ ◊ ▫

According to Jewish tradition, a boy becomes a man on the day of his bar mitzvah. My bar mitzvah was in May 1937. It was a big event for my family, just as it is today for Jewish families all over the world. My parents threw a large party, and relatives came from far and wide to celebrate with us. I was very nervous beforehand, but when at last I was called to read from the Torah I was surprisingly calm. My voice rang out confident and clear, pronouncing each Hebrew word flawlessly. I passed the test with flying colors.

The following year the Nazis overtook Austria and implemented their hateful anti-Jewish policies. My father lost his business, and I was kicked out of school. Over the next few years our family was torn apart. My older sister and her husband fled to Cuba; my father was imprisoned and sent to Auschwitz; and my mother and I went into hiding in France. Relatives and friends were hounded, tortured, slain. I managed to survive through a combination of luck, cunning, and the kindness of others, but I knew the Nazis would find me eventually—and I knew what would happen to me when they did.

In 1943, at the age of nineteen, I found myself high in the mountains of northern Italy with several other Jews. We were hoping to find safety in Italy, which had surrendered to the Allies. In the mountains we met a group of Italian army officers, who told us the Germans were moving in to occupy northern Italy. These men had no desire to spend the rest of the war in a Nazi prison camp, so they were going to take refuge in the high country and await help from the Allies.

Their plan sounded good to me, and I decided to join them. They gave me a gun and a uniform and restored my sense of dignity. For too long I'd been running like a frightened animal, totally dependent on others for safety. Now I had the means to defend myself from my enemies, to confront them face to face, to fight back.

Biancastella did many things that I, the bar mitzvah boy from Vienna, had never thought I would or could do.

Biancastella wore the same filthy, lice-infested uniform day after day. He foraged for food, eating berries right off the trees. He carried a gun everywhere, killed Nazi soldiers, blew up bridges and supply vehicles and power plants. He sat on military tribunals and condemned prisoners to die. He crossed Nazi-occupied territories to collect relief funds, shepherded supplies through the mountains in blizzards, lied his way out of traps.

In each new situation, I went through the same set of emotions I had felt on the day of my bar mitzvah: fear, followed

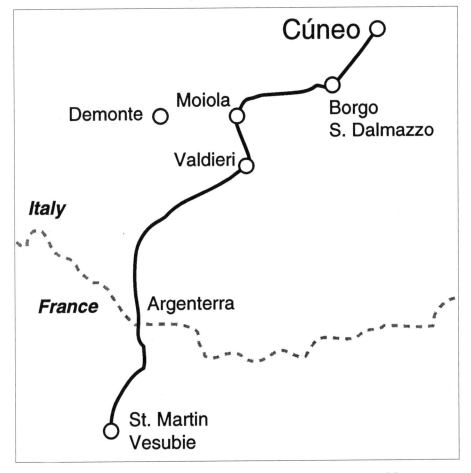

1. Map of the route into Italy taken by me, my mother, and hundreds of other Jewish refugees.

by an unexpected sense of steady resolve. Every test, it seemed, was more difficult than the one before. But I did what needed to be done.

◻ ◇ ◻

Biancastella means "white star" in Italian. There is considerable irony in the translation, for as Biancastella I was hardly a beacon of light; I was a saboteur, a killer.

But in another sense "white star" was a fitting name for a Jewish freedom fighter. It contrasted with the yellow stars the Nazis forced German Jews to wear during the Holocaust. These yellow stars identified the Jews as subhuman and were one of the many forms of humiliation and degradation the Nazis heaped upon us. I, unlike most Holocaust survivors, was lucky enough to get a chance to stick up for myself. After I became a Partisan I didn't have to accept the Nazis' arrogance and cruelty. I was no longer at their mercy. They may have conquered all of Europe, but they did not conquer me. And therefore they did not conquer the Jewish people.

So if the yellow star symbolized the persecution of the Jews, then perhaps "white star" symbolized our tenacity, our refusal to submit. Though a star may only be a faint speck of light in a pitch-black sky, enough stars remained shining through the dark night of the Holocaust that our people lived to see a bright new day. I and the thousands of other Jews who outlasted the Nazis were living proof that not even Hitler's Final Solution could extinguish the fire of Jewish pride, independence, and self-reliance.

1

How Sweet It Was: The Beginning

My life's journey began on May 10, 1924. My parents had been hoping for a son ever since their other child, a daughter, was born six years earlier. They named me Heinz Josef Burger.

I was born into a comfortable world. My affluent parents lived in a beautiful country and owned a fine home and a successful business. Both were raised Orthodox Jewish but were nonobservant as adults. My father, Elias, was born in Slozcow, Poland, one of nine children. His family immigrated to Vienna before the turn of the century, and life was difficult for them. In struggling to make a living, Grandpa Josef became involved in horse trading. Unfortunately, the nags he sold belonged to the Austrian army. After this happened, Josef went to America—as everyone in trouble with the law did. He intended to go to Detroit, Michigan, to join distant cousins who had immigrated earlier, but after he was screened on Ellis Island in New York, he became ill, developed pneumonia, and died shortly thereafter. He was buried in Queens, New York.

These events left the nine Burger children on their own, so at a very early age my father became the man of the household. Because he had flat feet, he was exempt from service in the Austrian army during World War I. He was fortunate to find a good job in a textile shop providing fabric for the army. By the end of the war, he owned a textile business in partnership with a dear friend. He also had married and become a father.

Here is how he rated his siblings. His oldest brother, Jacob, sat at the top of the list. He had become an attorney, and that was quite an achievement. Then came Julius; Dad admired him because he was a successful classical musician. The next oldest, Bernard, passed the bar and practiced law, and brother Salomon worked as a traveling salesman, mainly in Sweden. He was married and had four children. That was all for the honor roll.

The bottom of the list included Siegfried and his twin sister, Steffi, plus Isaak and Max. Siegfried was always in trouble with the law for minor infractions; Isaak was a small-time gambler; and Max did not amount to much, either. Steffi got married, had a daughter (Gerti), got divorced, and wound up selling pins, needles, and threads from door to door. Because these items were difficult to sell, she painted her teeth black and wore old rags on her rounds to elicit her customers' sympathy.

Theresia, my mother, was born in Vienna in the former Austro-Hungarian Empire. She had two brothers and one sister. Her parents were also poor; they lived two buildings away from my father's family. Her father struggled to make a meager living as a loan collector, going from house to house each month. Theresia studied music at the Vienna Conservatory, winning first prize in a Bach competition. When she met Elias Burger, she ended her music career, married him, and became a housewife and mother.

One of my earliest memories is of an event that occurred when I was about four. My mother took me to the city to visit my kindergarten teacher, with whom I was madly in love. But before taking the tram, we stopped at a local bookstore. The next thing I knew I was in a doctor's office, sitting in a chair, with ether in my face. When I awoke, the doctor was cutting something out of my throat. I started to feel pain, bit his hand, and cursed him. My tonsils were gone! Even worse, I had not seen my beloved teacher. This was the first time anyone had lied to me, and I felt terribly betrayed.

The ice cream my father brought home that night almost made me forgive the lies. Ice cream was a once-a-year treat in those days. But this was not enough. I was still in love with my teacher, and I was hurt. My father did the only thing he could do: he invited my kindergarten teacher to dinner, hoping she could talk me out of this infatuation. She agreed to come to our house. I was very nervous but fully prepared to propose marriage to her. She sat down with me and explained that this could never be: she was already married. I was not willing to share this goddess with any other man, so I had to give her up. This was my first taste of one of life's bitter pills: bonds are formed and broken, dear ones come and go.

2. Wedding picture of my parents, Elias and Theresia Burger, Vienna, Austria, 1917.

As a consolation gesture, my parents bought bunnies for me. The pets were kept in the garden, and our caretakers, who occupied the basement apartment of the house, tended to their needs. All I had to do was play with them. When my beloved pets grew up, they became harder to handle. One day I came to play, and they were gone. Mother told me they ran away to get married and have lots of little rab-

3. My great-grandparents,
Poland, late 1800s.

bits. However, I found out some time later that the caretakers had made a delicious stew out of them. I was crushed. How could humans be so cruel? How could killing be acceptable?

To make up for this horrible occurrence, my mother bought me a little white mouse. I immediately became very attached to my new friend. After a few days, I took him outside the house. On the fence sat a big cat. I recall going to the fence to show my little friend to the cat. That was the last time I saw my mouse; the cat had a good meal. It was then decided that pets were out for a while.

I was a rather solitary youngster. It was tough to make friends in my predominately Christian neighborhood. Only one kid would talk to me, so I was determined to make him my friend. On my fifth birthday my parents bought me a new kiddie car, a little red one with pedals. I was thrilled to death because my old one was at least a year old and a little banged up. The next day, when only the maid was home, I presented my friend with the greatest gift he had received in his short life—my old kiddie car. Such joy had to be seen to be believed. He was all over the street with his new toy. Salieri Gasse, our street, ascended a steep hill, and we lived at the top of it. When my friend rode the car down, it was quite a

4. *My father's parents, Clara and Josef Burger.*

5. *My mother's parents, Ilka and Ignatz Pories.*

6. My father and I in front of our house at Salieri Gasse 6, Vienna, 1930.

hike to come back up. I was impressed, because I was never allowed to ride in the street. That afternoon after one of

7. My father with the family car, a Styer 6, 1930.

his trips, I waited for him to come back up. What I saw was horrible. My mother was dragging the kiddie car up the street, and my new pal was in tears, following her. She had decided I was not entitled to make the monumental decision to give anything away—even if I had more toys than I could possibly use.

Naturally, I lost my only friend. In fact, I had created a fierce anti-Semite. Our family was now recognized as the only Jewish one on the street. At that time, it did not bother me too much. I did not know we were different, other than being rather affluent. Our lifestyle was privileged. My father had a car, a Styer 6—the only Austrian-manufactured automobile. He had become associated with a French textile company, Tiberghien and Fils, which had factories in Trencin, Czechoslovakia. My father and his partner became general representatives of this large operation and did very well financially. Then my father's partner died, and his wife became the new partner. She had two sons, Georg and Hans. Hans was a year older than I, and we became close pals.

My father was a passionate music lover and sportsman. He became a devoted patron of the Vienna opera house, concert halls, and theater. Almost every night was "music night." On Sundays he went to soccer games; his favorite team was Vienna Austria. My mother never joined him at concerts or sporting events, but her life was equally pleasurable. She paid a daily visit to her favorite coffeehouse to shmooze with women friends, then came home to supervise the maid in preparing our supper.

My older sister, Edith, was in school most of the day. I am sure she often would have liked to kill me. I used to tease her mercilessly. As the baby of the family, I could get away with it; I was a cute child, and my parents spoiled me rotten. Edith spent her leisure time falling in love with famous Austrian film stars. She had a formidable crush on Ernst Verebes, a Hungarian star. She became so obsessed with him that my father used his contacts to find this fellow at the studio and convinced him to have dinner with our family. My sister was terribly embarrassed. Imagine the letdown when he turned out to be a total cretin, although he was good-looking.

My grandparents were an important part of our life. My father's mother, Clara, was never very interested in grandchildren, but my mother's parents, Ilka and Ignatz, were loving and caring people. My Aunt Mimi lived with them. After one of our visits to my grandparents, Aunt Mimi decided to go home with us. We made a stop on the way home, and everyone got out of the car. Aunt Mimi accidently slammed the car door on my hand, crushing my fingers. I screamed my head off; it was so painful I soiled my pants. We rushed home, and the humiliation began. My clothes came off in the upstairs bathroom, the only one we had, and my behind was dunked in the bidet. This was totally degrading, because I knew this tub was

8. *My father's textile business in Vienna. Elias, my father, is standing to the right of the woman. I am in the foreground on the left. The tall man at right was Dad's chauffeur, who later became an SS officer and arrested Dad in 1938.*

9. Family vacation in Grado, 1926.
10. Grado, 1926.

for girls. I eventually overcame my humiliation, but I had a hard time forgiving my mother and Mimi.

I was rather accident-prone at that age. One day I irked my sister a bit too much, and she kicked me right in the butt, sending me flying through a glass door. I was hopelessly stuck, my neck encompassed by sharp, broken glass. I kept my cool and did not move. When my father came home for lunch, I was rescued without suffering any physical damage. My throat was not severed; I was going to live. Even better, my dad smacked my sister across the face with his newspaper.

One afternoon soon after this incident, I did not feel well, so my mother put me to bed. I told her my right side hurt, and she guessed that the problem was my appendix. She called Doctor Dedekind, a gentle physician who made house calls.

11. With sister Edith in Vienna, 1926.

*12. With sister Edith
in Vienna, 1926.*

Mom told me that if the doctor asked me if I hurt on my lower right side, I should tell him I had no pain. This ploy did not work. He touched me once, and I went through the roof screaming. He wrapped me in a blanket, drove me to the sanatorium, and promptly cut me open. My appendix had burst, and I was just minutes away from death. I had to stay in the hospital for a few days and had around-the-clock nursing, but nobody could make me happy until I was home again. Many times later I reminded my mother that she seemed to have wanted to kill me. Had I kept my mouth shut, as she suggested, I would have been dead.

More often than not, though, keeping my mouth shut would have been a good idea. I could be a real pest. I recall being extremely jealous every Christmas because Edith was always invited to spend Christmas Eve at her girlfriend's house. We never had a tree, so this was a real treat for Edith. I carried on until Mother forced Edith to take me along. I was an uninvited guest, so there was no present under the tree for me. I had a tantrum of major proportions. Finally, a small pocket calendar appeared, and I shut up. I never was allowed back for another Christmas.

Early the next year, Edith and a male companion wanted to go skiing in the Vienna Woods. Mother insisted that Edith take me along. I was a pretty good skier. When the time came to make my way back to the tram station, I took the trail and got to the bottom ahead of Edith and her friend. As I waited, I grew impatient. Not knowing what time it was, I thought they had left me. I had no money and could not make a phone call, so I decided to stand at the corner and beg. Almost immediately someone gave me ten groschen, the price of a child's fare on the tram, and I took the tram home. When I came back alone, the noose tightened around my sister's neck. She finally arrived, exhausted from searching for me. She tried to explain that I had probably perished on the slopes, and as much as she tried, she could not find me. Mother then took her to my room, where I was propped up in bed, resting comfortably with a cup of hot chocolate and a plate of cookies. Edith had a hard time getting out of this one.

My sister was always in trouble. She once cut school to go autograph hunting at film stars' homes. (I am sure the maids signed the photographs.) Whenever my father wanted to find Edith, all he had to do was go to the nearest movie house. Because she had usually charged the ticket, Dad would have to bail her out and take her home. After he yelled for a while, all was forgiven.

◻ ◇ ◻

Kindergarten was just about over, and I was getting ready to go to real school. I was scared. Others had warned that it was going to be hard and that I would have to learn to read and write—not only in script but also in *kurrent*, the German way of writing. School in Vienna was a whole-day affair, so at age six I became a very busy fellow. I would have rather played all day and had fun, but my parents had expectations of Edith and me. They had attained no small measure of wealth and privilege, and they naturally wanted us to be able to enjoy an equal degree of comfort when we grew up. I understood that education was a necessary evil, and I did what was required of me. Unless I was ill, I showed up every day—six days a week, with only Sunday off.

The good thing about school was that I was able to make lots of new friends. One of these was Erich, a big, clumsy Jewish fellow who lived not too far from us. His mother had a business

13. Vienna, 1929.

in their home. Erich's uncle, a polio victim from birth, lived on the top floor. He always sat on a chair that was also a toilet, which freed family members from having to help him all day. I recall that the whole family was unkind to him. He was yelled at frequently and had no way to defend himself. Even though he was totally paralyzed, I knew his brain was working normally. We kind of established a relationship; I was always kind to him, for which he was grateful. I was probably the only one who treated him well. I spent a lot of time at Erich's house, but somehow Erich was never welcome in ours.

My friendship with Erich didn't last too long. He told me he had met a nice gentleman in the park who offered him candy and cookies. All he had to do was let the nice man play with his sex organ and vice versa. That sounded very peculiar to me. I told my mother, who told Erich's mother. Everybody had a fight, and Erich and I were never allowed to see one another again.

But I soon found friendship from an unexpected source—my father. One day he asked me if I wanted to go to a soccer game with him. I was not too eager to give up my Sunday, but my mother insisted I go. I went, but not enthusiastically, although the thought of having my dad's undivided attention was quite attractive. At first Dad was very cross because he had trouble finding a convenient parking place. His

14. Vienna, 1929.

15. With pet rabbit, 1930.

mood brightened when we entered the stadium. We had great seats, right on the center stripe and about fifteen rows up. The Vienna Stadium was and still is a magnificent sports facility. The game was between the Vienna Austria and the F.C. Admira. My dad bought me a knockwurst on rye bread to amuse me. Little did he know I was becoming a passionate lover of the game of soccer.

From then on, Sundays were father-and-son days. My weeks became monotonous. All I did was wait for Sundays and the soccer games. I don't know if it was his intention, but Dad was showing me the eventual pay-off of those seemingly endless days of school. Season tickets, with seats right at midfield—that was for me.

I seemed to do all right in school. After class, I often went to a vacant lot with some fellows to push a tennis ball around and pretend to be a great soccer star—maybe Mathias Sindelar from the Vienna Austria. He was my idol. Every day I got yelled at because my shoes were dirty and wearing rather rapidly from the extra use. After all, soccer was a tough business.

Adulthood, I began to notice, was a tough business, too. Late one night, when I was eight or nine years old, there was quite a commotion downstairs. My Uncle Julius, the conductor of the Stuttgart Opera and my father's pride and joy, had arrived from Germany. I overheard from the top of the stairs that Julius was always exaggerating and that he should never have left Germany in such a hurry, leaving everything behind.

Julius explained that my father did not understand what was going on there and that the Jews were in great danger with the new Nazi Party in power. My dad gave his brother some money, and we all went back to sleep.

Soon after, Father made a fast trip to Germany to make a few purchases. Inflation was so overwhelming that he was able to buy a large corner house in Berlin and bring home a big car—a Daimler, which was probably the equivalent of a Rolls Royce. To me it seemed as long as a city block. The only problem was that it did not fit in the garage. So, as much as my dad loved this new toy, he was forced to sell it. Later his building in Berlin was taken away because it was Jewish property.

Our house in Vienna was also in danger, but not from the Nazis. My dad's brother Jacob, the attorney, got in deep trouble with the law. He made collections on behalf of his clients but neglected to finalize the transactions. He spent the money himself, with the help of his mistress, Nettl. A meeting was set up in our house. The screaming and crying went on all afternoon. We kids were not supposed to know about any of this, but we could not help overhearing. Jacob faced disbarment, and my father, unwilling to let this dishonor befall our family, dutifully agreed to bail my uncle out of his predicament. Jacob turned over all his jewelry and valuables, and my dad sold the house.

He rented a magnificent apartment for us in the ninth district. It once belonged to the imperial family, which used it as a stopover. The building had three floors. We had the first, which had been the living area; the second had been the sleeping quarters for the imperial family, and the third floor had been the sleeping quarters for the help. All the floors were occupied by Jewish families. I recall that the dining room area was enormous. It should have been used as a riding academy. Dad had a platform built for our baby grand piano, which looked tiny in the corner of the room.

I did not have my own room anymore; a divan was set up for me in my mother's bedroom. My dad set up sleeping quarters in the *herrenzimmer*, the gentleman's room. He had a magnificent mosaic inlaid desk, bookcases, armoires, and a great leather couch in this enormous room. In addition, he had a new modern bed with a telephone next to it. I even recall the number: A 20–2–28.

It was easy to see that my parents had physically separated. I guess divorce was never considered because of what the neighbors might say. Life in our family became a real pressure cooker. My dad took Edith under his wing, and my mom got me.

I began spending less time at home. I continued to go to school in Gersthof, and rather than going straight home I often stayed to play soccer. When the match was over, I'd spend my transportation money on something to drink and usually had to walk home. I had only a few believable excuses as to why I was so late and finally had to admit what I had been doing. I was in instant trouble. My mother was a first-class hitter. One never knew when and where a blow would come from.

The school year ended, and vacation time came. Mother, Edith, and I went to Siofok on Lake Balaton in Hungary. It was nice there—good swimming. Mother insisted on cooking all the meals on a small Sterno stove in our room, which was disappointing. If we had wanted Austrian food, we might as well have stayed in Austria. The only entertainment for me, besides swimming, was an afternoon program at the main hotel in town. It was a children's show, performed by some very talented youngsters. I loved it. Because Mother would only allow me to attend one time, I got into the habit of lifting the price of a ticket from my mother's purse. Eventually I got caught, and I was grounded for the remainder of the vacation.

While we were gone, Austria went through a political

crisis that nearly led to civil war. The Nazi Party organized an uprising, and the army was called in to put it down. Troops were shooting at workers, and the government almost collapsed. The rebellion finally failed, but this experience really shook the country.

When I was ready for middle school, my folks enrolled me in a private school that Dad's partner's sons, Georg and Hans, attended—the Schottengasse Realschool in the first district of Vienna, a twenty-minute walk from our house. It was a tough school. All of the teachers were professors, and the hours were long. I'd had it pretty easy so far and enjoyed great privileges without having to put out much effort. Now, I realized, I'd have to shape up.

My first disaster was religion class, one of the main subjects. My instructor, Professor Frankfurter, a relative of U.S. Supreme Court Justice Felix Frankfurter, was very strict. Religion was taught twice weekly; about five classes were combined because there were not enough Jews, Catholics, or Protestants in just one class. We had about thirty students in this class. Professor Frankfurter read the roll call the first day of his class and slid the little tabs into position on his class layout. Everybody always had to sit in the same chair. By looking down, he was always able to know everyone's name. He picked his teeth with a gold toothpick.

He invited the class to speak freely and to ask questions if we were in doubt about anything. Then he started to teach about Adam and Eve and the Garden of Eden and the snake and Abel and Cain. Not realizing what I was getting into, I raised my hand to offer what seemed a simple and logical statement: "If Adam and Eve had two sons, then Eve had to sleep with both of them to make more people on this earth. Therefore, it seems to me that we are all bastards."

Frankfurter stood up, pointed his stubby, fat finger at me, and screamed: "In the corner, Burger!" He was foaming at the mouth. For the whole year, I never left the corner. I never learned a thing about religion.

The rest of the subjects were okay, although I had some difficulties with math and history. Fortunately, I received some help from a tutor, who turned me into an "A" math student overnight. It cost Dad a few shillings, but it was worth it. With history I struggled a bit longer. I could not wait for the year to end.

I knew now that my dad had a mistress. She was his business partner, Frieda Weiss. In my opinion she was really ugly, but she was a powerful woman who always pushed my dad to move up in the world and to better himself. She was a top-notch bridge player, and Dad learned the game. He was lousy at it, but he loved it. Frieda—we called her Fritzi for short—accompanied Dad frequently to the opera, to soccer games, and, I presume, on vacations. My mother was livid, in part because Fritzi had once been her best friend. Mother's favorite name for Fritzi was "tramp."

At this same time, Edith was dating a young man named Duno Tendler, whom my dad had brought home. He was studying medicine at the Vienna University of Medicine. He had a glorious operatic baritone voice. Dad took him under his wing and talked him out of becoming a doctor. He clothed him, gave him money, and ultimately sent him to Milan, Italy, to study voice. Because of this, our next vacation was to be in Italy.

The three of us arrived in Milan and were met by Duno. As usual, my dad took his vacation in Bad Gastein or at some other spa. He claimed to be arthritic. We visited Milan for a bit, and seeing the cathedral was first on the list. Duno was denied entry, not because he was a Jew but because he was not wearing a jacket. I thought this was very funny. He lived here, and he should have known better. We also visited the Galleria, a marvelous array of fashion shops from all over the world. I was thrilled. The best part about our short stay was lunch, where I was first introduced to risotto Milanese, a marvelous rice dish.

On we went to the train station and north to Stresa, a famous tourist town on the Lago Maggiore. Only rich people could afford it. We went on to a tiny town just north of it, a typical Italian village. We got one room for the three of us. Mother immediately set up the kitchen: out came the Sterno, and good old Viennese cuisine was ready to be produced. We all loved Italian food, and none was better than that in Italy, but it was not to be.

The lake was beautiful. In its center was a lovely island, Isola Bella. It belonged to the king of Italy, Vittorio Emmanuele. Lemons and oranges grew on trees, something I had never seen before. We went to visit it by boat. I did some swimming, mostly alone. Some Italian kids came around, and I desperately tried to communicate with them. I wanted to play some soccer. I said "fussball"; they said "calcio." We meant the same thing but never knew it, so there was no soccer.

About the middle of our stay, Duno came to visit one day, and we got to have a meal in a local restaurant. I ate everything on the menu. One local fellow tried to pick up my sister. He wanted to impress her, so he showed her what he had in the trunk of his convertible. It was a bidet. Her face was very red, and Duno never stopped laughing.

It was a very boring vacation for me. Only one wonderful thing happened during our visit to Italy. I must mention it to explain the marvelous attitude of the Italian people. One evening the road company of the Scala of Milan Opera House set up across the lake in an ancient Roman coliseum to present *Aida* by Verdi. We were spellbound. The voices were great. The house was packed: women with infants nursing, men in their Sunday outfits. Everybody was totally engrossed in the music; not a single child cried. I made up my mind that I loved Italians.

16. Wedding picture of Edith and Duno Tendler.

□ ◊ □

When we returned to Vienna, I learned that our Chancellor Dollfuss had been kidnapped by a bunch of Nazis. The kidnappers came on the radio and announced that Austria now had a new government; the Nazis were in power, and a new leader would be chosen soon. The military intervened and restored order. Unfortunately, Dollfuss was killed. Kurt Schussnigg became the next chancellor. He did not wear military clothes, so it seemed to me that he was much classier-looking than our previous leader.

Soon it was back to school. My second year was a lot harder than the first. I could already sense a great anti-Semitic feeling toward all Jewish pupils. We had only a few Jewish professors. I worked very hard, but my efforts seemed to be useless. The biggest problem was French. For any German-speaking person, this language was totally foreign; the structure and pronunciation were totally different from what we were used to. It became clear almost immediately that without after-school help, I was not going to make it, so a tutor was hired to help me.

I was still in big trouble with Frankfurter, my religion professor. He told my father he would definitely flunk me unless I became bar mitzvahed in his synagogue. In addition, he wanted three cuts of wool textiles for suits, and an associate rabbi was to become my Hebrew instructor. The synagogue in question was in a different part of town, and my grandparents, who were Orthodox and would not ride on the Sabbath, would have difficulty getting there. Frankfurter did not care. I don't think my dad wanted me to have an Orthodox ceremony, but religion had become a main academic subject in Austria at that time, and I would have to repeat a year if I flunked the class. So we agreed to Frankfurter's demands.

The teacher rabbi was almost as indigestible as Frankfurter. He, too, had a golden toothpick, which he used constantly. It seemed to go with the profession. The fact that I did not comprehend the Hebrew language did not disturb him at all. He simply made me memorize the whole service. This cut severely into my regular study time, and I found myself faltering in all of my classes. My test grades were usually just above failing. I was also unwilling to give up any playtime, and I therefore found myself confronted with certain disaster. But I always squeaked by somehow.

Often, while sitting in the rabbi's dark room, smelling the garlic aroma, I dreamed of the good times I spent in our house. When my grandpa came to visit, he walked this long way; because he was Orthodox, he would not ride. Grandpa was a strong man. I remember him climbing our cherry tree to pick cherries for me. I did not have the heart to tell him they were inedible. I recalled the once-a-year ice cream parties in our garden. The ice cream was homemade and delicious, and I can still taste it.

After a severe warning from school officials and a talking-to from my mother, I pulled my act together and started to study harder. I think the greatest incentive was an offer to be the student of the week. This student was given a free ticket to a midweek soccer game. I finally made it and came home to announce this incredible feat to my mother, only to find her crying her eyes out. My Uncle Moritz, the jeweler, was very ill, possibly near death. It was probably blood poisoning. His wedding ring had become too tight, so he had decided to cut it off;

the pliers had slipped and nipped his finger, and gold dust had entered his bloodstream.

Mother forbade me from going to the game, but I went anyway; it was a well-earned reward. When I returned home, I learned that my favorite uncle had passed away. My mother was too crushed to hit me for my disobedience. I felt bad enough anyway. Uncle Moritz was a classy individual. He had been an appraiser before owning his successful jewelry business. He and his wife, Grete, loved Edith and me very much. I recall that for every birthday, we would receive a gold piece, which my dad promptly put in the safe to keep for our future.

My whole life now revolved around school and studying. I applied myself more than I had before. Math was no problem for me, and I received superior grades. History was still difficult. Now they added geography. European boundaries had been badly butchered after World War I, with the old Austro-Hungarian Empire dissected into small pieces, and I had a hard time putting all the pieces together again. Geography was the only major subject that might create a year-end problem. If I flunked it, I would be condemned to another vacation of study (something like summer school) and makeup tests in the fall.

I also became more involved in my Hebrew education. It was oppressive, to say the least. To offset this ordeal, I was allowed to join the Boy Scouts, an experience that was quite enjoyable for me. I met new boys; we had meetings and went on field trips. I worked hard to graduate from Cub Scout to Boy Scout. I passed all my tests and finally made it. I was very proud. But when my overcoat was stolen at one of our meetings, Mother immediately banned me from future participation.

However, I had my heart set on going to a huge jamboree that had been planned for some time. All the troops were to meet in the Vienna Woods. Defying my mother's wishes, I went. All I needed was car fare and courage. I returned home late that night. I had no key to get in the front door. If you had

no key, you had to ring the care-
taker of the building. There was a
charge for getting him out of bed.
I rang the bell and woke Mister
Matushek. As he let me in, I
looked up and saw that my mother and father were both at the window waiting for me. Not only was
I in trouble for going to the jamboree without permission, but my
dad had to pay the key money to
get me into the house. This was
officially the end of my scouting
career.

My sense of independence
was growing, but so, it seemed,
was my penchant for trouble.
Summer was approaching, and I
was getting very upset with
Frankfurter. Even though I was
guaranteed passage of his course, I
still had to stand in the corner. He
had never forgiven me for my

*17. Grandmother Clara with
daughter Steffi in Vienna, 1936.
Steffi was a twin and the youngest
child.*

comments about Adam and Eve. I decided that, with the nice
weather, I should take a little vacation from religion class. For
the next three weeks, I spent that hour in Votiv Park. It was
nice there—no pressure. Of course, the school administrators
became interested in my whereabouts and sent somebody to
my house to ask questions. My mother was called to the principal's office and told of my truancy. I remember coming down
the stairs in school on that infamous morning just as my mom
was coming up. We met in the middle, and I recall being hit
with great force. She pounded my head with her pocketbook;
I thought I would never regain my ability to walk or think. The

worst thing about it was the humiliation I suffered in front of my school pals.

Summer vacation that year was boring, just Mom and me at some Austrian lake. When I returned home, I began to prepare for the big year of my bar mitzvah. Jewish boys supposedly became men at age thirteen. I really started to look at girls now. If I was to become a man, I thought, maybe I would get to see a girl naked. We had no dirty books or magazines then; everything was left to the imagination.

In late fall I went on a ski trip organized by my school. I left Vienna from Westbahnhof, headed for Mariazell, a tiny village in the mountains. To get there I had to change to a little train. I still remember the sign above the window: "The picking of flowers is forbidden while the train is in motion." On the trip to paradise, I got a little tired and lay down on the bench. I awoke suddenly and found someone sitting on me: a rather well-developed girl slipped and landed on my face. It was my first scent of a woman. This girl had breasts and everything. I was thrilled.

After the ski trip I asked the girl for a date. She accepted, and we met. I had no idea what to do or how to behave. I was very shy, and I just took her for a walk. I was not quite ready for this; she was not the one I was going to see naked. I bid her goodbye and never saw her again.

Chanukah came and went—as usual, without presents. I would have liked a small Chanukah gift. Anything would have been fine. But we simply did not practice our religion. My mother went to synagogue only on the highest holidays. Yom Kippur was the most sacred of these. She was always prepared. She took a lemon spiked with cinnamon to prevent her from passing out from hunger. She went to the same Orthodox temple that my grandfather went to morning and evening every day of his life. Women were in the balcony. When Dad and I picked Mom up in the evening, she invariably had a

18. My bar mitzvah photograph, Vienna, May 1937.

brutal headache, supposedly the one that would be the death of her. When we arrived home and sat down to a supper our maid had cooked, she always recovered and promised to live another year.

My only involvement with religion was my bar mitzvah preparation. Because of my grandparents' Orthodox way of life, I was warned that only perfection was acceptable. Duno, who had come back to Vienna and started a torrid courtship with Edith, sometimes tutored me. He was smart; he was also from a very Jewish background. I never cared for him too much, but I accepted all the help I could get.

In addition to prepping me for my bar mitzvah, Duno helped me through another male rite of passage: he and his friend from medical school, Schechner, took it upon themselves to teach me about sex. I told them I knew it all, that we boys at school had researched the subject extensively and were all quite knowledgeable. Naturally, I enjoyed talking about sex with the mavens from the medical field. Duno told me that when he was in school he and his friends used to go out for lunch, hire a prostitute, and play gin rummy on her naked belly or butt.

Hiring a prostitute was one thing; sleeping with my sister was quite another. He and Edith got caught in bed together by my dad. From the next room, I overheard a lot of talk about dishonor, the shame of the family, and marriage. Sure enough, Edith and Duno were wed, though I do not recall a wedding; that's how quietly it all happened. Suddenly I had my own room, and Edith was no longer at home. She and her husband now lived in Italy, where he returned for more voice training.

Meanwhile, Mother acquired a "boyfriend," a Hungarian living in Vienna. This was convenient because Mother spoke fluent Hungarian. Nobody could understand what they were talking about. It turned out that Mr. Winkler was a married man with a daughter about my age. It did not really matter because I am sure nothing ever went on between them. My mother was not interested in sex. She needed the company, so she played the game. I am sure she wanted Dad to find out and become jealous, but it never happened. She tried to pull me into this arrangement; I was supposed to like this man. He was a publisher of sports books, mainly about soccer stars, and he gave me some of my idols' biographies. He even took me to the Vienna Austria's training session and made the players autograph the books for me. Still, I did not like him. He was what we called a Hungarian "gallerist," a first-class show-off.

My relationship with my dad's girlfriend was pretty good. She took me shopping, and I got new shoes, a new suit, knickerbockers, two pairs of pants, and one jacket. I always wore out the jacket before I could even get to the second pair of trousers. Knickerbockers were tough because they had a habit of falling down. They looked terrible, and I hated them. I was patiently waiting to get my first pair of long pants. It seemed I had been wearing the same pair of leder-hosen since birth. They were all glossy and stiff, like armor. When I took them off, they stood on their own wherever I left them.

I went to my mother's parents' house as often as I could—usually after school or Saturday afternoons. Anytime I needed money to buy chocolate bars or any other sweets, my grandmother Ilka always gave me one shilling. I got only one-tenth of this amount a week from Mother as my allowance, so the extra money went quite a long way—usually to the candy store. My grandpa was very angry about this. He always asked Grandma for money, and she never gave him any. But I never had to ask Grandma for the money. My mother never knew about this. I had to promise to keep it a secret.

My grandparents lived on whatever Mom could get for them. Dad did not make any allowance for their support. He knew Mom was lifting funds from the household budget for her parents. Her brothers, Moritz and Kobi, who were both well-off, also contributed. After Moritz died, things got a little tight, so Aunt Mimi learned to make leather gloves, eking out a meager living, and was able to help out. So Grandma was really sacrificing by giving me money. I knew all this but felt no guilt.

Fritzi Weiss and her sons moved from the eighteenth district to a new apartment in the first district that was located above the business. This was the inner city, a very elegant address. It must have cost a lot of money. It made Fritzi's commute to work rather speedy and easy—just an elevator ride away. I went to visit occasionally—without my mother's knowledge, I hoped. I liked to hang out with Hans. We went to the same school, and we usually got along very well. We had the same interests but rooted for different soccer teams. I loved the Austria; he loved the F.C. Vienna. I could live with this. It only became a conflict when the teams met head-on.

My Uncle Siegfried was in jail a lot in those days. He stole my grandmother's overcoat on a yearly basis; the cops usually found him hiding under his bed and took him away. He got six months, and the guards were elated to see him again. He had beautiful handwriting, and he always worked in the prison office. They treated him well, and with Grandmother's food packages every Sunday he made out all right. Uncle Isaak was smarter. He, too, was involved in the overcoat caper, but he never got caught. He had a different hiding place. Dad always replaced Grandma's coat just before winter to make sure it did not get stolen twice in one year. Grandmother was quite content to have Siegfried in jail. This way, she said, she knew where he was, and he could not get into any additional trouble.

Uncle Bernhard, while still in law school, secretly married a Catholic girl named Annie, who came from a very poor Viennese family. Bernhard came home for lunch every day, hoping that his mother would not find out about his secret wife. Eventually he had to come clean and explain why he had not slept at home for over a year. Lots of crying followed this revelation; the family was now infiltrated by a *goyte*, a non-Jewish person. But after a little time, Annie was accepted and loved. She truly loved Bernhard. She converted to Judaism and was promptly rejected by her family.

Uncle Julius, the musician, was back in Vienna. After his escape from Nazi Germany, he had gone to New York and worked for the Metropolitan Opera as a music coach for most of the singing stars. His wife, who was still in Stuttgart, wanted to join him in America. She sailed over, and he was called to pick her up at Ellis Island. He denied knowing her. She was sent back to Germany, went crazy, and was put into an asylum. Julius liked his attorney's secretary. She was young and very pretty. After his divorce was granted, he asked her to marry him, and she accepted. She became my Aunt Rosl, and I immediately liked her a lot. Nobody knew they were going to get married. Dad found out the day of the ceremony. Like all Jewish weddings, this one had to be registered at the *kultusgemeinde*. Someone called my dad at work and told him one of his brothers was getting married. Not knowing *which* brother, Dad got in touch with Grandma and asked, "Who got dressed fancy this morning?" The answer was Julius.

Later, Julius went to London, where he got a terrific job with the BBC. He became the arranger of their monthly musical extravaganza, which featured music from around the world. Dad listened to the program faithfully every month on his super radio receiver, which was powerful enough to receive Radio London.

◻ ◊ ◻

My twelfth year brought the death of my beloved grandmother Ilka. She had a bad fall getting out of bed one morning and broke her hip. She was confined to her bed for a long time and eventually contracted pneumonia, which proved to be fatal. Everybody was crushed. She was a very lovely lady, kind and gentle. I was not allowed to be present at the funeral because of my tender years. Grandma's death really hurt. It took me a long time to get over this loss.

My grandfather was left alone with Aunt Mimi. Now eighty-four, he spent most of his time in synagogue and at his favorite coffeehouse, which he was always on the verge of being thrown out of. He never played cards but was always kibitzing and giving away everybody else's hand. He also smoked very strong, smelly Italian cigars—reason enough for being asked to leave. His advanced age saved him every time.

My Hebrew studies went well. I had the whole ceremony memorized. Mom told me I had to be perfect. My grandpa counted on me. I loved him dearly and was not about to let him down, so I went through the torture. I could take it—only five or six months more.

I befriended a boy in my class named Gradisch. He seemed to know a lot about Adolf Hitler and spoke to me often about this famous leader from the north. I was not very impressed. Gradisch gave me a car battery so I could use the detector radio my grandfather had given me after Grandma's death. It worked great. Vienna had only one radio station, so it was easy to find the right spot on the selection board. I am probably the only person left who remembers this type of receiver, the forerunner of the vacuum tube radio. I used my little machine every night before falling asleep until the battery went dead. Nobody helped me get it recharged, so my radio days ended.

I was asked to join our class soccer team. That got me out of school once a week. I was always the smallest member of my class, so nobody took me seriously. One teammate helped me a lot. He was called "Neger," Negro. He looked like a very light-skinned African. All I knew about Negroes was what I learned from Tarzan books, which I loved to read. Neger was probably half-white and half-black. We did not care, because he was a terrific soccer player and won many games for us. I was not good, but they kept me around because I was a prankster. Whenever a joke was to be played on one of our professors, I was elected. I was good at this. I was never caught, never guilty. So I was part of the clique, and I loved it.

I hated my classes, though. My studies in French were still not satisfactory. I felt my grades were going down the tube because I was Jewish. Most Jewish students seemed to experience the same problem. So Dad hired a tall Aryan substitute professor to help after school. My grades miraculously improved enough for me to pass all my tests.

Father did not care if I spoke French, anyway. My future was already mapped out in his mind. After finishing realschool, I was to go to tailor school for four years to become a master tailor. Dad and I were to start a new kind of business. At that time in Europe, ready-made men's suits only existed in Dad's head. The idea was to start a manufacturing plant that would produce men's garments of all sizes, much as Robert Hall did in the United States. Dad was to provide the textiles, and I would run the plant. My future was assured. Nothing could go wrong. I would grow wealthy and eventually become a Viennese playboy.

This path to adulthood seemed clear as I stumbled into my third year in school. I felt as if I had been the victor in an impossible battle, overcoming a slew of obstacles—my own wayward behavior, anti-Semitism, and the dastardly Frankfurter—to reach the threshold of manhood. The truth was that all adversaries had been bribed or bought. That did not matter to me. All I had to overcome now was the last great hurdle: bar mitzvah.

□ ◊ □

In early January, Dad took me to his tailor to be measured for a man's suit—a double-breasted navy blue outfit with long pants. I got a man's hat to match the suit. Uncle Kobi, who owned an exclusive haberdashery in the inner city, was contributing everything else I needed. When it was all together, I went to have my picture taken. Many poses were submitted, and finally a few were chosen. I was as happy as I had ever been. It was great to be the center of attention. I was having the time of my life. I was sure it could not get any better. And I was nearly right.

Arrangements were made for a big party at my home. Mother was baking all kinds of small Viennese and Jewish pastries. Chairs were rented to accommodate all the invited guests. I hoped for a lot of expensive gifts and maybe even money. After all, with Grandma's death my money supply had grown tight, and my allowance was still a meager ten groschen a week.

The great day arrived on the second Saturday in May 1937. I was to become a man at last. The pressure had built up for so long I was ready to explode. I dressed in my new clothes, with my parents supervising every move. I think my father could have done without the whole ritual, but he had no choice. This was all for the benefit of the family, especially grandparents. My father picked them up on the way to the synagogue. Aunt Mimi joined the group, and we all arrived in Rabbi Frankfurter's domain. This was the first time I laid eyes on the place. It was a quaint and rather attractive building. I was hot and very nervous. What if I forgot my lines? Nobody would ever let me live it down. I rationalized that I did not even know what I was saying and hoped nobody else would, either. I neglected to acknowledge that this was an Orthodox congregation.

Finally, I found myself up front. I held on to the podium for dear life. But once I got going, the fear left me, and I began to enjoy myself. All those awful lessons had paid off after all.

Then I looked up and saw my grandfather, and horror struck me. He had fallen asleep during the services, as he always did in synagogue. I raised my voice but could not rouse him. Well, at least he was here and presumably happy. He would be proud of me, anyway. Afterward I was presented with a set of *twillem* and a prayer shawl—as if I had suddenly become Orthodox. Everything had gone well, and my family was pleased with my performance. I was pleased, too—mainly because, at last, the wrath of Frankfurter was lifted from my head.

In the afternoon the guests arrived at the apartment. What a disappointment. Except for two kids my age, all the invited guests were ancient—members of the family I didn't even know. They came just for the food. Worse yet, almost everybody brought a book as a gift. A few days later, after all the excitement died down, I found a local bookstore that was willing to take all those dull volumes off my hands. I got more money than I had ever had and somehow was never questioned by either Father or Mother about what had happened to all those great gifts.

The only other items I received were one fountain pen and Dad's present—a solid gold Longines pocket watch with a blue gem on its backside. It was gorgeous. My father presented it to me with a measure of pomp and ceremony. In spite of his skeptical attitude toward religion, I believe he felt somewhat proud on this day. I felt proud, too, but even more I felt a sense of relief. The monotony of school, the endless studying, the exams, the humiliations of Frankfurter—all this was behind me. My new timepiece seemed to beckon me forward; ahead lay new experiences, new rewards, the entitlements of a successful adult in a civilized society. Little did I realize how short the time had grown.

Dad let me look at the watch for a while, then took it away and put it in our safe. I never saw it again.

◻ ◊ ◻

Now that I was a man, my brother-in-law, Duno, tried to get me to pray every morning. When he detected my total lack of interest, he quit, and I became a kid again.

It was just as well. I flunked history again and had to study all summer to make it up. I was not about to go to public school, as my dad suggested. I was comfortable at the private school and did not want to change. I crammed all summer and passed my fall exam. All I had to do now was to finish one more year and I would be out of school for good.

Things seemed to get easier. The last year was almost like a condensed version of all the preceding years. Everything sounded familiar, and I seemed to roll along. My professors did not agree. It became clear now that Jewish pupils were being discriminated against. When I thought I did well, my grades were terrible—just high enough to pass or low enough to fail. The harder I worked, the less I achieved. Even French, though I was still getting after-school help, became harder and harder to conquer. My tutor, Herr Schamer, told me during one of our sessions that he was a card-bearing Nazi (which was at that time illegal in Austria). This statement made absolutely no impact on me; all I wanted to do was pass French. Herr Schamer later became a *sturmbandführer* in the Totenkopf SS.

But by the end of 1937, there was a definite Nazi presence everywhere. The SA stormtroopers in their brown uniforms attacked groups of people, and it was no longer safe to be outside at night. Usually, theater and opera patrons were targeted for brutal beatings. Dad stopped going to the opera for a while. He said you never knew when somebody would beat you up.

As time went by, Nazi pressure increased. I learned that Germany wanted to annex Austria. These were difficult times for our government. Most people, it seemed, did not want a Nazi takeover. To ease the pressure, Chancellor Schussnigg confidently ordered a plebiscite—March 15, 1938, was the date. The vote was to decide once and for all whether Austria would remain as it was or enter the Nazi fold. It was generally accepted that the Nazis did not have a chance to win. The whole country was in turmoil. I went to quite a few rallies. We were taken out of school and bussed to Vienna Stadium. Sixty thousand kids yelled and screamed, and none knew what they were shouting about. Occasionally we were taken to a Nazi rally. I thought the Nazis put on a better show than the government did. Their events were very colorful and well organized, and their propaganda was much more powerful than the government's. It never occurred to me what a catastrophe a Nazi victory would be for our family and for all of the Jews in Austria.

The city was divided between swastikas and the red and white flags of the Austrian government. I thought this looked kind of pretty. My dad was very optimistic about the outcome of the referendum. He was proud to wear the national colors on his lapel. Mother did not care about politics. Duno and my sister, Edith, returned to Milan; Uncle Julius returned to London. They were the only ones in the family who had somewhere else to go. Dad assured us that we had nothing to worry about. It was absolutely impossible that the Nazis could win. The poll showed a large majority for Schussnigg and Austria.

Suddenly, Schussnigg abdicated, and on the evening of March 12, 1938, the German Wehrmacht crossed the border. By the next day Austria was no more.

And just like that, I became a German Jew.

2

The Changing of the Flags

The German soldiers were received with great adoration—flowers everywhere, unmatched joy. Every new German was filled with happiness. Almost everybody in the streets was in some kind of uniform, wearing the *hackenkreuz* on his or her left sleeve and greeting passersby with right hand raised, yelling "Heil Hitler," the new salute. I was overwhelmed. It was like a dream. A very bad one.

Austria was now the Ostmark, the eastern province of greater Germany. Arthur Seyss-Inquart was the new *gauleiter*, handpicked by the führer. He was a high-ranking SS man, a notorious Jew-hater. His job was to cleanse the Ostmark of all undesirable elements as soon as possible. Dad did not think it was going to be so bad. He was assured by his employees and "friends" that we were all quite safe, that Germany only wanted to rid itself of Chassidic Jews, who lived mainly in Vienna's second district (which the Viennese called "Jew Island"). The word was that these undesirables had come to Austria from Eastern Europe without permission. They lived as a cult and were no longer welcome. They would be "asked" to return to their homeland. That meant they would probably be put into a ghetto somewhere in Poland. Everyone else would be left alone. My dad and most assimilated Viennese Jews were lulled into a false sense of security; they wanted to believe this tale of Nazi propaganda.

I met my pal Gradisch the day after the annexation. He wanted to see me, to give me his new salute and show off his new uniform. We walked for a while, and he stopped at every store window that exhibited Hitler's picture. He asked me if I did not think this man was beautiful. I sincerely thought Hitler looked like a maniac and was ugly. I omitted the word *maniac* in my answer, but otherwise gave an honest reply. Gradisch turned abruptly and left with hatred in his eyes. I was lucky he did not belt me. By the time I got home, he had thrown a good-sized rock through our living-room window. That evening, Dad told me to hold my tongue and never to insult a Nazi.

The schools reopened after all the celebrating had died down. I was led to the principal's office and told I had been transferred to the nearest public school. Schottengasse Realschool was off-limits to Jews. The principal gave me the papers and information I needed to register in my new school. I did not go home first; I was sent directly to the new location and registered. As soon as I entered my new classroom, I was attacked by what seemed to be the whole class and beaten to the floor. They called me a *saujude*, a swine Jew.

By the time I got home I was totally destroyed. My dad told me to take it easy; things had to get better, he said. He was right, sort of. After I endured two more days of beatings, the Jewish laws were introduced in the Ostmark, one of which stated that Jewish children were no longer allowed to attend school. I was expelled, and my education was over.

At first I was elated. What thirteen-year-old would not have been? No more classroom boredom, no more studying, no more routines. But I soon realized that this was no good, either. There was nothing to do, nowhere to go, no one to play with. It sunk in rapidly. I was marked, a Jew. I stayed home a lot.

Dad seemed to accept this new life. He did resent certain aspects of it—for example, Jews were banned from plays, concerts, operas, soccer games, and other public events. But to offset all of this, my father's business blossomed. Good woolens were almost impossible to purchase in Germany, and Dad was selling everything he could lay his hands on. He was making a lot of money, and he was allowed to keep it all—for now, anyway. Just to play it safe, we got an affidavit from a distant cousin in Detroit, Michigan. Such a document had to be submitted to the U.S. consulate as part of the application for an immigration visa. We knew by now that we could not stay in Nazi Germany indefinitely.

Every Jew had to put up with a lot of brutality. The front page of the *Sturmer*, a Nazi propaganda sheet and the only legal newspaper in Vienna, always had caricatured close-ups of three Jews. The individuals in these heavily retouched pictures looked like Tasmanian devils—long noses sucked up by deformed mouths, black Chassidic clothes all dirty and ripped. The headline was always: "Look at your enemy; defend yourselves." This paper listed all the Nazi exploits: how many Jews were arrested, how many deported. At night the Hitlerjugend wrote anti-Nazi slogans in the street with chalk. In the morning they picked up Jews going to work, usually better-dressed people. They gave them a brush, a pail, and water, then forced them to get on their knees and scrub until everything was clean. This was daily entertainment for the people of Vienna; even the Jews viewed it as a laughing matter. I failed to see the humor.

It was decided that I would learn a trade. If we were able to get to America, I would need some way to make a living, and because my regular education had been halted I enrolled in a school for electricians. My dad bought me a pair of overalls so I would look like a laborer when traveling to and from class. I looked stupid; I was a little guy in work clothes. Who were we fooling? But I took the train every day and "worked" from nine in the morning to three in the afternoon. At least it passed the time.

My cousin Fredl was in officer's training in the Austrian army at the time of the Anschluss. When Germany overran Austria, he was given the uniform of the Wehrmacht; he was now in the German army and wore a swastika on his chest. He was plenty scared, and soon after the Nazi takeover he appeared in our apartment in full uniform. On that day, the SA went from house to house to conscript Jews for scrubbing duty and other menial tasks. The doorbell rang, and two brownshirts wanted Jews. Fredl opened the door, and everybody yelled "Heil Hitler!" The Nazis apologized and left after a few jokes. Fredl was hysterical. He had to keep them from finding out that he was a Jew in a German uniform, for which they could have killed him. Soon thereafter, he was quietly discharged and returned to civilian life.

◻ ◊ ◻

My fourteenth birthday was uneventful. More and more Jews were committing suicide, as many as two hundred a day. The Nazis persecuted Catholics, too. One morning a troop of SS entered a monastery in the center of town. They chased all the priests and nuns to the top floor of the building and made them jump into the street. According to the *Sturmer*, nobody survived. This was considered a great Nazi triumph. There was no religion of any kind in this land. The only bible was Hitler's book, *Mein Kampf*, which he wrote while he was incarcerated after World War I. It was a guide to hatred and murder, outlining the creation of the master race and eventual world domination.

My darling Aunt Annie was an angel, interrupting my boredom quite frequently. She used to pick me up at home, put a little golden swastika on my lapel, and take me and Uncle Bernhard to a for-Aryans-only swimming pool. Bernhard looked Aryan, and as long as I wore a swastika, I was okay. Had we been found out, it would have been a different story. I might have gotten away with it, but Annie and Bernhard would have been arrested and shipped to Dachau.

Annie, who was the only non-Jew in the family, volunteered to act as a messenger between my father and my brother-in-law, in Milan. A lot of money, jewelry, and cameras left the country with her help and were later recovered by my parents. Dad took all the gold coins Edith and I had received as presents over the years and had cigarette cases made from them. Annie got them all out, one by one.

Once Annie came to the house and showed us a blank baptism certificate she had been able to lift from her priest's office while nobody was looking. She wanted Bernhard to become Christian the easy way. All she needed was somebody to fake the priest's signature. I was an accomplished forger, having faked my mother's signature many times while in school. Annie produced a document with the priest's signature on it, and I used my foolproof method. The signature was traced with a soft pencil, preferably a number-one grade, onto a piece of parchment paper. Then I peeled a hard-boiled egg and rolled it gently over the tracing. The signature was now on the egg. Next I rolled the egg over the certificate. A faint image of the signature was now in place. All that was left to do was to write over that image with ink. Voila! Annie typed in all the information needed, and Bernhard was now a Christian. The funny thing about this was that Annie had previously converted to Judaism, so they still had a mixed marriage. The Nazis never found out about it.

The U.S. consulate in Vienna informed us that our waiting time for an immigrant visa was quite a bit longer than expected. We were classified as Polish citizens because my dad had been born in Poland. They knew we were Austrians, but the United States used a quota system based on the family patriarch's place of birth, so we went on the Polish quota, which lengthened our waiting period. Fritzi and her two sons were in better shape because they were considered Austrians.

I found a way to make a little money at this time. I met a travel agent who was able to procure visas to Shanghai, China. The price was reasonable, and a lot of people were buying. I found several interested families, got them together with this Hungarian fellow, and received a nice commission for my effort. The strange thing was that the visas were legitimate, official documents, not fakes. People were able to get out of Germany with them. Dad was not interested in going to China, though. He could never learn the language, he said. The truth was that he was much too busy making money to think of such a move.

Six months after the Nazis had become masters of our country, things had not gotten any better. My grandfather liked to sit on a park bench on the Danube canal and look at the boats and talk to anybody who cared to listen to him. One morning he came to relax on his bench. He was about to sit down when he saw some writing on it—*Juden verboten* (Jews not allowed). He thought about it, went back to his apartment, got a chair, placed it next to the bench, and spent his morning undisturbed and happy.

Our apartment became a haven for lost Jews. Out-of-work musicians who were friends of Duno's used to visit frequently and entertain us. This was really nice, because they were professional performers. My dad helped a lot of them get out of the country. Some had visas but no money. They came to Dad for help, promising to repay him later, when they had a new life. Dad just nodded his head. He did not expect anything from anybody. In his own way, he saved a lot of lives.

I got fatter and fatter, in part because I had no exercise. I stayed at home most of the time rather than venture abroad and risk a beating. To relieve the boredom, I spent some time rearranging the electrical wiring in the apartment—not always successfully. We had 220-volt DC current in Vienna. That's powerful stuff. I attempted to put new lines into the walls. However, during my three months of "schooling," nobody had told me that the wires had to be run in insulated tubes. Moisture eventually ate through the wires and created spectacular fireworks. I never paid any attention to the potential danger. I just ripped everything out of the walls and replaced the fuse, and we got our power back.

Dad got permission from the Nazi authorities to send a crate to the United States. Our piano and assorted lightweight beds were picked up to be shipped to Uncle Julius in America. He had been promoted to assistant conductor at the Met in New York. Our place looked empty with the piano gone.

□ ◊ □

On November 7 a young Polish Jew, upset over his parents' deportation to Poland, shot a German diplomat inside the German embassy in Paris. The Nazi propaganda machine went into high gear immediately. The radio station broadcast anti-Jewish venom from morning to night. The next day's *Sturmer* was full of hatred. On November 9 the Nazi died.

Nazi leaders whipped their followers into a frenzy. Starting at six in the evening, Nazi units raged through the city, methodically ravaging and vandalizing Jewish properties. Kristallnacht was upon us. A Jew's life was worthless. I saw Jews being brutally beaten, then carried away by laughing SA or SS men. (Most were taken to local police stations for deportation or shipment to Dachau or Buchenwald.) The Nazis conducted door-to-door searches for Jews. It was up to the concierge of each building to tell them where the Jews were living, how many were at home, and who should be taken away. Our concierge was good to us, and no Nazi came to arrest us. We were very lucky.

My cousin Fredl stumbled in, totally dazed. He looked very Aryan, so he was not attacked. He stayed with us for a short while. Dad did not come home that night; we did not know if he was still alive or how long this nightmare was going to go on. We tried to stay away from the windows, hoping no one would see us. I don't think my mother understood what was happening. It all came to an end at six o'clock on the evening of November 10, after twenty-four hours of terror. The phone rang. It was Dad; he was safe. He had been able to hide in the attic of his business building. Fritzi and her boys were with him. Later that night, Dad came home.

There was no more illusion of our being able to stay in Vienna. A few days later, Hitler gave a speech addressed to the whole world. He said that all the countries that thought Jews were so great should take them off Germany's hands. He said what the world had just witnessed was only the beginning. If nobody wanted to relieve him of the Jewish menace, the Nazi Party would have to find a different solution.

Nobody abroad paid any heed to these poisonous words. It was up to the Jews in Germany to find a way out. Almost 30,000 Jews were already in concentration camps, to be released only if they could produce an entry visa into some other country. My dad was finally ready to talk immigration. He had had the foresight to buy a counterfeit Greek passport for Edith and Duno shortly after the Anschluss. Edith came back to Vienna for a few days after the takeover to pick it up. She went back to Italy as a Greek citizen. The fake document was outstanding and held up until they got to Cuba, in 1941. Dad also urged Bernhard to go to Italy and await his American visa there. He did go and was spared the terrible experience of Kristallnacht. He received his visa in March 1939, and he and Annie arrived in the United States in late April.

19. My father's passport.

About two weeks after Kristallnacht, my father went downstairs as usual to go to work. He was met by his chauffeur, who was wearing an SS uniform. The man arrested Dad and Fritzi and had them jailed in the Rossauerlande, a small prison usually used for inmates awaiting transfer to larger institutions. We received no information regarding the charges against them and could not communicate with them. They languished there six weeks, then were given a choice: either sign Dad's business over to a Nazi executive or go to a concentration camp. The choice was obvious. They both came home unemployed.

We were still a long way from getting U.S. visas, so a second way out of Germany had to be found. Edith and Duno had gone to Nice, France, with the help of their passport. It was decided that France would be a good stepping-stone for us. All it took was money. Duno made contacts in Italy and France to make an illegal entry possible. It was a good plan.

In the beginning of 1939, all Jews were moved into small areas. Most ended up in the second district, Jew Island. All Jewish property was auctioned off. In less than two hours, all our belongings, furniture included, were sold for about two and a half U.S. dollars. Even that paltry return was not ours; it had to be donated to the Nazi Party. The Nazis confiscated all my father's financial assets, too. But Dad was a step ahead of them—he had a substantial Swiss bank account—so he did not worry too much.

We had to relocate to a small apartment, which we shared with two distant cousins. Time did not go by quickly; I was bored stiff. I had some money left from my visa dealings, and I purchased a small camera. Dad bought me a small enlarger and some trays. One of the cousins had some knowledge of photography and taught me how to develop film. Photography occupied all of my time now. I was no good and did not know what I was doing, but I was happy. I decided that this was going to be my profession.

In the beginning of March, we were finally ready to apply for a passport. We set about obtaining the necessary documents—namely, a certificate showing that all taxes were paid in full and that none of us had a criminal record, as well as a document issued by the Kultusgemeinde attesting that we were full-blooded Jews. All four grandparents had to be Jewish; Germany was not issuing passports to Aryan men, who were not supposed to leave the Reich. I presume they were drafted into the Wehrmacht or some other fighting force.

The day at the gestapo was totally dehumanizing. There was a long line of Jews waiting to get passports. Every Nazi walking by had abusive words for us. Some spat on us; some swung sticks and hit us. This lasted the whole day. I was afraid we might have to come back the next day, but by evening we had been issued passports of the Third Reich. The cover bore a swastika on brown paper. The first page revealed another swastika in the center, and right next to it on the upper left was a large red "J," the mark of the Jew. They made sure that wherever we went we were recognized as *untermenschen*, subhumans.

It did not matter. We had to have papers to leave the country.

3

The Immigration

In April 1939 we boarded the train to Italy, the first stop on our flight to France. No visa was required for this leg of the journey. Italy was allied with Germany, part of the Axis. We were allowed only one suitcase and twenty reichsmark per person. When we got to the border, we endured one more moment of humiliation, one more display of Nazi cruelty. The Germans held us up, checked our passports, and made anti-Semitic insults just to intimidate us one last time. Finally, they turned our baggage upside down, and everything fell to the floor of the compartment. They left laughing and very proud of themselves.

The Italian border guards followed, helped us pick up our things, welcomed us to Italy, and wished us a happy stay. I said to my dad that maybe they did not realize we were Jews. But they did know; they simply recognized us as human beings.

We arrived in San Remo that afternoon. Edith picked us up at the train station. It was so nice to see her. As we strolled along the boardwalk in the sunshine, gazing over the Mediterranean Sea, a new feeling of freedom came over us. I was ready to forget all the brutal things I had witnessed and lived through. Just being here was a new beginning. We had a terrific Italian meal, took a walk on the boardwalk, and felt good all over. Suddenly the spell was broken: A group of Nazis came into view. It was Hermann Goering and his entourage. They were having a good time, joking and laughing, and they paid no attention to us. I was so surprised that I forgot to be scared. I wanted this to be my last look at a Nazi. I was sure there were no Nazis in France, our eventual destination.

We made our first attempt to cross the border the next evening. We were driven somewhere into the hills, and Italian *bersaglieri*, mountain fighters, were to lead us into France. The attempt failed. Supposedly the wrong French guards were on duty that night. We returned to San Remo and waited for a new route to be found. Fortunately, there were plenty of them, although some cost a little more than others. The one finally chosen for us was the easiest and most expensive. A Russian scientist owned a piece of property on the border. The estate was half in Italy and half in France, and the owner was rarely there. A taxi would be waiting on the French side to take us to Nice.

In the afternoon we ran into a man named Goldstein, which was a big surprise for Dad. He and Goldstein had been in jail together in Vienna. Dad told him how we expected to cross the border, and we all joined forces. We were driven to Ventimiglia, the Italian border town. At about eleven at night, we went to the gate of the property and made our entrance. We were on our own now; no guide was part of the deal. We were all scared, because Germany was still on our minds. We did not want to get arrested. The path was gravel-covered and crunched noisily underfoot as we walked. The sound seemed especially loud at night. Goldstein kept whispering, "Elias, we haven't been in the can for a long time!" We seemed to have gotten lost. There was no exit gate in sight. After what seemed an eternity, we came to a metal fence and saw the Mediterranean coast on the other side.

We climbed the fence and slid down a lamppost on the other side. Since I was the youngest and considered the most able to perform this feat, I went first. Goldstein was next, and he made it well enough. Mother, who was not very athletic, ripped her slip and complained a lot. Dad came last.

The promised taxi was nowhere in sight. We walked down the street toward our right; my geographic knowledge from school told me Nice lay in that direction. Shortly, we came to a bus stop. The sign on the bus waiting there read "NICE." We were in France.

We boarded the bus, afraid that if they found out we were all foreigners we would be arrested. It seemed that was all we ever thought about. The Nazis had trained us well. But we were safe; nobody did anything to us. We bought our tickets on the bus and rode to Nice. We arrived late at night, took a taxi to Duno's apartment, and rang the doorbell. Duno slept like a log, and we could not awaken him. Even a stone or two on the window had no effect. We found a hotel two blocks away and summoned the courage to ask for a room. Goldstein knew a few words of French, and we got a room, no questions asked.

We got Duno up first thing in the morning, and he took us to the police station, where immigrants were processed. Duno knew a policeman who for a few francs would provide the documents we needed to stay in the country legally. This officer was a little man who seemed to have no authority at all, but he held our fate in his hands. He sent us across the street to have our pictures taken in a small photo studio that looked like a cave. The owner introduced himself; his name was Jean Nocenti. I would get to know him very well.

We got the pictures rapidly, took them back to the station, and were issued permits. The permit was a green piece of paper with name, birthplace, and, most important, nationality. They called us *ex-Autrichien*, ex-Austrian. I felt greatly relieved to shed Germany from my identity document. This permit was supposed to be only temporary. In a few months, if we were good people, we would get a permanent document, a carte *d'identite*. Green was the color for self-supporting tourists; this was not a work permit. We had to renew our document every month and show we were able to live on our own money. My

20. My father in Nice, France, May 1939.

sister was notified by telegram that everything went well and that she should pay the Italian people who had arranged our passage.

Duno had already rented an apartment for us in the same building in which he lived. A large wooden crate stood in the middle of a closet. My dad saw it and smiled broadly. I don't know how or when he did it, but he'd packed the crate full of his suits and shirts and shoes and sneaked it out of Austria. As a textile man, my father placed great importance on his clothes. He owned thirty custom-made suits with matching accessories. He used to wear a different outfit every day. I had never noticed anything missing from his closet, but here it all was. He was Mister Burger again, and I was happy for him. He immediately asked Duno to hire a carpenter to convert a small room into a very large closet with racks to accommodate all his suits.

I thought for a while that Dad and Mom were trying to get together again. They shared the same bedroom. But a few days later, we received visitors—Fritzi and her boys. I didn't even know they had left Vienna. I could spot some venom in my mother's smile. Fritzi, Hans, and Georg were supposedly on the verge of getting their U.S. immigration visas. They were lucky.

Hans took me around to show me the town. He went to a grocery store and picked up a couple of free passes to a show. All the gambling casinos had free revues every day. People went to see the show, and during intermission the drapes were pulled back to reveal the gambling tables. Everybody gambled during that time. Hans and I entered the Casino de la Jettee, a magnificent domed building on pillars overlooking the Mediterranean. A show was in progress. Some guy was singing, and on each side of the stage there were three gorgeous girls, totally nude, standing like statues. My eyes were glued to them. I decided I was going to spend all my time in here. For the next few weeks I established headquarters there.

I met a young German who owned a photo store in town, and he offered me a job after I told him about my interest in photography. He knew I did not have a work permit, and he did not care. The French never enforced this requirement, he told me. I had to work six days a week for free, just to learn the profession. On Sundays I watched the store, sold film, and took in work, for which I earned ten francs, about two and a half dollars. I was elated, and Dad was happy for me.

The first Sunday found me alone, minding the store. My first customer was a woman who spoke only French. I spoke only German. After trying unsuccessfully to communicate with her in sign language, I racked my brain, and all my French lessons from Vienna came back to me. My tongue loosened, and I spoke my first words. It was all easy after that. I heard nothing but French all day and was fluent in no time.

My dad made me give him half my income. I was able to go to the movies once a week with my half. I was happy. My boss, Herr Foglar, was a young, handsome ladies' man. He always had enlargements of his girlfriends in the nude hanging around the lab. I loved to look at them. I was really ready for sex but did not know how to go about it or where to find a willing partner. I was very shy. I was sure Hans had already lost his virginity, because he bragged enough about it, but he was not willing to share the secrets of sexual courtship with me.

One day I met Fritzi on the street. She proudly showed me her passport and her American immigration visa. She said their passage was booked and that they were leaving soon. I looked at the visa and was very unimpressed. I don't know why I was not happier for them. Maybe I was jealous.

The family moved to a new apartment—Boulevard Gambetta 74 bis. We had the second floor, and Duno and Edith occupied the third. Duno was offered a contract by the

21. My father in Nice, France, May 1939.

Monte Carlo Opera House, and he gladly signed. His name was changed to Daniel Duno, a name that stuck with him until his immigration to Cuba. The opera season did not begin until late fall, but his impresario, Mr. Sirota, arranged for two concerts, one in Nice and one in Monte Carlo. I was not sure how successful they were. These were insecure times, and with world peace hanging in a precarious balance, people were not too tempted to go to some unknown's concerts.

In August Duno and Edith moved to Fontainebleau, a town about thirty miles south of Paris. The royal palace was its main attraction, and the forest was the other. By the end of August, my parents were convinced that it was best for the family to be reunited. We moved to join Duno and Edith, although only temporarily. Dad left most of his cherished wardrobe in Nice. Edith found an apartment for us on the top floor of a house. The first floor was a kennel, and the barking never stopped. The fact that we all liked dogs did not make it any more pleasant. But it was a great location, just on the edge of the forest.

I was kind of glad to give up my job in Nice. I had gotten a little tired of working such long hours without decent pay. I was hoping to be in America soon, and there I would get a real job. In the meantime, I would enjoy being lazy.

It was a short-lived vacation. War was imminent.

□ ◊ □

On September 3, 1939, World War II began.

I recall the speech by French president Edouard Daladier. He said the French and British had declared war on Germany, that the German leadership had made a terrible mistake by attacking Poland, and that the German people would have to pay the price. The Allied armies were going to make this a speedy affair. I felt all warm and patriotic inside. I felt like a Frenchman. Tears came to my eyes when they played the "Marseillaise" at the end of the speech. I was elated that the Allies were finally going to stop Adolf Hitler and his Nazi brutes.

French propaganda boasted that the *bosch* would be crushed within three or four weeks and that Allied troops would soon march into Berlin. If the Nazis were going to be defeated, as the French promised, we could all go home and resume our lives. It was with great hope that we waited for developments.

The first night, at one in the morning, the air raid sirens went off. The sound was terribly loud and piercing. I almost fell out of bed. Chaos reigned in our place. We had been told that Germany had used poison gas during the last war, and we thought they might do so again, so we ran into the woods and tried to find a high point close to the town. Supposedly the gas would not rise but would sink to the lowest point. I was so frantic that I put my pants on the wrong way. My shoes were left behind, too. I was really scared. I was not ready to die.

The alert lasted three hours. The all-clear sounded and we went home, tired but elated that the German planes had not reached us. The next day it was announced that the sirens would go off every time an enemy plane crossed the French border. The previous night's alarm had been raised by nothing more than a small reconnaissance aircraft. Two more nights of sleeplessness convinced us that we needed to move again.

Only half the country was within the alarm radius, so we went to Vichy to await the Allied victory. It was a gorgeous place, a world-famous spa. People from all over the world came here to get healthy. The famous Vichy water came sparkling and warm right out of the ground. It was recognized as a healing liquid for all kinds of ailments. I never took a bath in it, but I sure drank a lot of it. I did not notice any change in my health. We stayed in a pretty fancy hotel in Vichy and even had our meals at the hotel restaurant. My dad did not let my mother cook in the room, for which I was thankful.

Our easy life did not last long. The French government issued a proclamation that all aliens born in Germany and Austria would have to be put into a camp for screening. Nothing was said about how long this would last. Men over eighteen were targeted. My dad was sent to Gurs, a facility close to the Spanish border. Nobody knew anything about this place, but Dad did not mind. After all, the war was going to be over shortly.

Meanwhile, Edith announced that she was pregnant. After much debating, she and Duno decided she should have an abortion. People in their right minds would not bring a child into the world during wartime. A midwife performed the operation, and Edith came through it all right. Duno was happy to have it over with, but I was not so sure how Edith felt; she had always wanted to have a baby.

I found a job in a local photo studio. They did photo finishing, with which I was quite familiar. It took a lot of talking to convince the boss to let me work there. When I mentioned casually that I did not expect to get paid, I was hired—foreigner or not. I figured that if I did a good job, he would throw a few francs my way. I only stayed a few weeks, though. The war was dragging on, and it seemed to be taking longer than planned to beat Germany, so we all returned to Nice. We got back to our apartment and resumed our "normal" lives.

Duno and Edith were able to secure Cuban visas and get away from this war. The Cubans demanded a large sum of money as landing security. I was sure my dad had taken care of this small detail before his internment. Meanwhile, I looked for a job. My old boss, Foglar, was no longer in business—he had probably become a prisoner of war—but I found employment very soon in a large photo finishing plant. I even got paid a small amount. After all, I was an experienced operator now. During the day I helped in all areas: developing prints, drying and sorting them, and getting the envelopes together. In the afternoon I had to deliver the finished work to the appropriate stores. We worked for thirty-one stores in Nice and three in Cannes. They gave me a bike and a little suitcase, and off I went. It was fun. I got to know all the people and made a lot of friends.

The war went on and on. Both armies sat behind their respective defense lines, waiting for the other to make a move. The British sent troops as rapidly as they could mobilize and train them. It seemed that a repetition of World War I was in the making—trench warfare. Then, right around my sixteenth birthday, Germany launched its western offensive, and the roof fell in on us. All aliens were banned from border areas and sent to other locations in France. Mom and I were sent to Biarritz. When we arrived there in the middle of the night, the authorities told us we could not remain there. Biarritz was located on the Spanish border and was therefore off-limits to foreigners.

We were pointed toward a small town named Auch in the wine country of southern France. We finally found a room. At this stage of the war, aliens were not received with open arms, especially in a small town like Auch. My mom never learned to speak French, so she was always thought of as a potentially dangerous foreigner. She did not care. Out came her trusty Sterno cooker, and we ate Viennese meals again.

The country fell into chaos. Refugees were on the roads everywhere trying to escape the advancing German forces. Planes from the Luftwaffe sprayed bullets all over the homeless people, killing many. The Allies were losing the war. I had a feeling big trouble lay ahead if the Nazis continued to advance. The news came fast and furious, even in our little town. The British almost lost their expeditionary forces in Dunkirk. Fortunately, they managed to evacuate a lot of men.

Auch was located approximately seventy kilometers west of Toulouse. I was prepared for the worst. I expected to see Nazi troops at any moment. Were they going to carry on as they had in Austria, I wondered, or were they just going to occupy France, content to have won this war, and eventually return home? In my mind, now that France was on the verge of disaster, Germany might turn against England and leave us alone. Finally, the announcement came that the *bosch* were in Paris. The newspaper had a picture on the front page of Hitler and his Nazi troops marching on the Champs Elysees. The French army had unconditionally surrendered to the Nazis. The armistice was signed, and the war was over.

To my relief, the Nazis only occupied the eastern half of France. The south was to be left alone; it would be called the unoccupied zone but had to obey all German demands. I did not know what those demands were at that time, and I really did not care. The mayor of Auch came to see my mother and me and announced that we were free to go back to Nice. He hugged us and bid us goodbye. I think we were the only immigrants in town, and he wanted to get rid of us. We took his advice and returned to Nice.

The next day, to our happy surprise, Dad came home. He had been released at the end of the war. The French did not want to be caught with German-speaking prisoners, so all Nazis and Jews were sent home. We later learned that the prison camp was very close to Auch; we could have visited had we only known. Dad was only a little the worse for wear, a bit thinner and terribly dirty. The accommodations in Gurs were far from sanitary. He was lucky to return to us in decent health.

We resumed our lives as well as possible, and Dad renewed his quest for U.S. visas. Jews were no longer liked in France; we were not persecuted per se, but we were always in danger of being sent to Germany as laborers. The Germans offered the French a deal: for every three "volunteer" laborers sent to Germany, they would return one prisoner of war. The Nazis had captured close to 2 million men after the French capitulation. To complicate matters, we still had to renew our permits every month, but now we had to prove we had enough money to live on without working. The few Jewish families remaining in Nice had a cash fund of ten thousand francs, which circulated among us whenever we were summoned for renewal. The French police bought it. Our little officer was still in the same department and was a great and loyal contact. He would alert me if we were in danger of being deported.

I got my job back at the photo plant. Monsieur Corbasson, the boss, must have liked me. He was not afraid to hire an alien. I was happy to work again. In addition to my old duties, I was now in charge of deliveries and pickups in Cannes. I was given bus fare, and off I went. The trip seemed to take forever. The buses were running on wood because there was no more gasoline to be had. The Nazis had taken it all. I could go faster by bike than by bus. It was thirty kilometers each way, mostly flat terrain. I was given the bus fare anyway, as a bonus. I made this trip three times a week.

I was still a virgin and not happy about it. In July one of my coworkers, Jean, told me he was going to solve my problem. He took me to a house north of the railroad station and told me to have ten francs in my hand and knock on the door. My heart was pounding, but I realized it was now or never. I was about to grow up. I knocked; the door opened, and I almost ran away. The apartment was four steps down, and the woman inside looked like a dwarf. She couldn't have been more than four feet tall. I pulled myself together, stepped down, and faced a lady in her thirties. She wore a robe, and her hair was not combed. She asked me for the money. While I was paying her, I tried to explain that I had never done this before. She seemed pleased about that. She assured me that there was nothing to it, that I was not going to get hurt, and led me into the next room. She lay on the bed, opened her robe, and told me to take my clothes off and lie on top of her. Everything I had wanted for so long started to happen. It did not take long. She told me I had done well and said to come back anytime. I was now a man of the world; after this experience, I felt, nothing could hold me back.

In November Dad and I had to go to Marseilles to renew our German passports. The Swedish consulate handled the German affairs. We went by train and received a one-year extension. We had to wait quite a while for our train, so Dad and I had a rare chance to spend some prime time together. While we were talking and strolling around town, I spotted two good-looking hookers. I tried to convince my father that this might be a great way to pass the time while we waited for our train departure. I was sure he would have liked to have done this, but he declined. These women could be ill, and if we couldn't pass the physical for our American visas, whenever that might be, we would be in sad shape. We returned to Nice as pure as we left.

We might as well have indulged; our American visas were nowhere in sight. Dad, getting impatient, decided to try to get us Cuban visas. He sent a large sum of money to Duno in Cuba for this purpose. But Duno apparently used the money instead to procure Cuban visas for his impresario and the impresario's daughter. I had known all along that Duno was very selfish, but I didn't realize how far that selfishness would take him. So far I had not learned how to hate, but I was learning fast.

In October Dad bought three counterfeit Cuban visas. The price was steep—$3,000. I remember how happy he was when he came home to show off the documents. But as we looked at them more closely, we were horrified. They were done so poorly that nobody could have possibly been fooled into thinking they were authentic. Dad was angry and yelled a lot. He left the house and went out to find these criminals and get his money back. That was the last time I saw him as a free man.

The French police had already arrested the counterfeiters. Dad and seven other victims were asked to go to the police station to file a complaint. They all went. Once there, however, they were not permitted to speak; they were arrested and jailed, while the crooks were set free. The prefecture in Nice advised me that they had no choice in the matter; this was now the law of the land. Any Jew somehow connected with a criminal offense had to be detained, guilty or not. They told me Dad would get his day in court eventually. An attorney was recommended. Mother sent me, as the man of the family, to see the lawyer. She told me she would get the money somewhere. This had to remain a big secret; nobody was supposed to know she had access to money.

Monsieur Augier was a young, understanding lawyer. He showed compassion and was not a Jew-hating man. He thought there was no case against my dad but recommended that, because of these difficult times, we hire a big-name attorney, someone a judge would be afraid of and respect. We retained Moro-Giafferi, the most famous lawyer in France. He had represented the unions in 1934 and had won the forty-hour workweek, among other things, for French workers. Monsieur Augier found him somewhere in the unoccupied zone. He accepted my dad's case; the trial was scheduled for March 1942. That meant Dad and the others would have to stay jailed for six months.

In December the United States entered the war. For us, this meant little. The Nazis still appeared to be winning on all fronts, and it looked quite hopeless. I went to see my dad every Sunday. He looked thin, and his head was shaved. They let him keep his own clothes, which made him feel a little better. We tried to get some food for him, but it was very tough.

Jews had reduced ration allowances, but we always came up with some treat.

I had to quit my job in the lab; it became too risky. I went to the movies one day and met the owner of the Cinema Olympia, who was somewhat impressed with my story. His name was Jean Marell. He told me that in a few weeks, the movie house was to be closed for alterations; he was going to make it larger. I did not understand this; the house was never filled to begin with. But it was his money. After the work had started, I was kept pretty busy with all kinds of chores. Jean and his wife, Marie, were happy with me and told me that if it ever became necessary, they would gladly hide my mother and me for as long as necessary. That made me feel terrific.

Dad's trial date finally arrived. Monsieur Moro-Giafferi entered the courtroom without even talking to Dad or me. He presented his case, and the judge immediately annulled the whole thing. All eight men were to be set free. The charges were dropped. I was totally flabbergasted; surely it could not be this easy to get a Jew freed. It wasn't.

I went to the prison that night to get my dad. He did not come out. The next morning was the same. I went every time they released prisoners—twice a day. On the third day I went to the Perfecture de Police and was told Dad was not to be set free. As a Jew, he had to be confined in a holding camp. When I said that he was found innocent, I was told to shut my mouth and stop being funny. The eight men were to be sent to Vernet. Not much was known about this camp except that it had a reputation for bad health conditions. Inmates slept outside, the tents were broken down, the food was practically inedible, and communication with inmates was almost impossible.

On the third day following the trial, I went to the prison to see my dad and the other seven prisoners, all of them inno-cent men, being led away in handcuffs by two gendarmes. It had been four years since the Nazis had come into our lives, and now it had finally sunk in: our lives were definitely at stake. Up to now, it had always appeared that the situation was not so bad. I was always able to adapt easily and never worried about deportation or loss of life. But that terrible prospect had now become all too real. Once a Jew had gone to Germany, he or she did not have a chance.

Dad was loaded on a streetcar. The eight prisoners were all standing on the rear platform of the car. I followed on my bicycle. When they arrived at the train station, the gendarmes took them directly to the train. In those days anybody entering the station was issued a pass, which permitted the bearer to exit without being questioned. There was a little time before departure, and I was able to convince the gendarmes to remove Dad's handcuffs since he was an innocent man, not a hardened criminal. The gendarmes agreed; in fact, it looked as if they wanted to give us a chance to get lost. The gendarmes went inside the car to do something. Dad and I were alone. This is our chance, I said. I begged him to run for it. I would lead the way; I knew how to bypass the train station security. But Dad refused to run. He said he had done nothing wrong and therefore had nothing to fear. The eternal optimist had spoken. I was able to embrace him before the train left the station.

I never saw him again.

All attempts to get him out of Vernet failed. Monsieur Augier was informed that Dad had been transferred to Drancy only one week later. He was now in the occupied zone.

I tried to put Dad's deportation out of my mind, but it was impossible. Mother never comprehended the severity of all this; she lived in a dream world. In the unoccupied zone, women were not subjected to the German demands for workers—not yet, anyway—so Mom never thought about it at all. She still went to a local coffeehouse to schmooze with her few remaining friends. It seemed nobody cared about them at all. They all spoke German; none had mastered French.

With my father gone, we moved out of the apartment into a furnished room. The landlady was a crippled woman in a wheelchair who looked out the window all day. Her husband wore an SOL uniform, which meant he was a French Nazi. They rented to us even though we were Jews; our money was still good, and times were tough.

I was spending a lot of time with the Marells. The cinema was going to reopen soon because the alterations were almost completed. I could not see how the new setup was any different from before. People just entered from the opposite side now, and the screen was on the other end of the theater. But Jean was elated. The movie booked for the grand opening was *Le Juif Suss*, a German anti-Semitic propaganda movie being shown all over German-occupied territories. It ended with a very bad Jew being hanged. The film was very popular. I sensed that the French people had become quite anti-Semitic. Despite all their hatred of the German conquerors, the French were quite ready to accept the Nazis' anti-Jewish doctrines. Given a chance, I felt, they would be just as cruel as their masters.

I was very uneasy. My eighteenth birthday was approaching rapidly. At that age I would be qualified for assignment to the work camps in Germany. I still did not use the word *deportation*. I told myself two months of work in Germany would not be the end of the world, knowing full well that Jews never returned from there. I almost considered myself French. I spoke the language perfectly, had no foreign accent, and was totally assimilated. But these things meant nothing at all. What mattered was that I was Jewish.

On my eighteenth birthday my mom and I were called to the police station for renewal of our permit. My contact policeman came to the house to warn me. He said not to show up, to go into hiding somewhere and stay there until otherwise instructed by him. He was going to tell me when it was safe to come up for air, if ever. This lifesaving information cost us one thousand francs. It was well worth it, too. I told Jean what was happening, and he said, "Get your things, only necessities, pick up your mother, and get your behind into my apartment. You will be quite safe here. I am a member of the SOL; nobody will suspect anything."

I was overwhelmed by this generous offer. Mother did not understand why she had to hide, but after I convinced her that she, too, could be deported now, she came along. We were officially off the police blotter. We had disappeared and were no longer the French authorities' problem.

The Marells did not ask for any money. Mother slept on a cot in the dining room. I was given a small room Jean had used as an office. The couple had their own bedroom. The rest of the apartment consisted of a small kitchen, a bathroom, and an entrance hall. It was very beautiful. We had not lived in such a place since Vienna.

After a few days, Jean took me aside to talk to me seriously. He said there was only one condition for his letting us stay there. He explained that he had a very good-looking girlfriend and that his relationship with Marie had become impossible. According to him, she was a nymphomaniac, and he was unable to satisfy her sexual desires. "You are going to seduce her," he said. "It won't take much. She is always hot as a pistol. She will do it with you; she told me as much. She said she could really enjoy such a young stud." I did not know what to say. I just nodded my head, and he shook my hand and wished me good hunting. He was free of her and went to his mistress to tell her the good news. I was very excited. Never before had I been called a stud.

I was awaiting my first chance to be alone with Marie. With my mother in the next room, it was not easy to become a

Casanova, but it happened. One afternoon I was sitting on my bed in the office, and Marie came in wearing only her robe. She sat beside me, and before I could even react she was nude and on top of me, kissing me and taking my clothes off. I was really in a different world. This was a beautiful woman who wanted me. I forgot that my mother was in the next room; it did not matter. We made passionate love over and over again. Every morning, after Jean left for work, I would join Marie in her bed. This was a dream come true. Every afternoon we had a matinee or two in my little room. I never got tired of it.

Marie cooked all my favorite meals. She must have spent a lot of money to get all this food on the black market. Mother and I had no ration cards. Marie made sure I ate well, because she wanted me strong and able to perform at any time. As time went by, Jean came home less and less frequently, sometimes not at all. Marie couldn't have cared less. She was happy.

Whenever Jean came home he wore his French Nazi uniform. He told me rumors were floating around that the Nazis were just about ready to occupy the rest of the country. The situation could become tricky. For now I was in heaven, my every desire more than satisfied. But hell lay just around the corner.

4

In Italian Custody

On November 27, 1942, the mirage of security evaporated. Jean came home and told us to get out. The Germans were on the way, and he refused to be caught hiding a couple of Jews. Mom and I were out on the street, and the SS were on the way. We returned to our furnished room and sat there, helpless, expecting to be taken away very soon. Our Nazi landlord was waiting to point his finger at us, hoping to get a medal. I was numb with resignation. Mother and I had been abandoned to our fate, and it seemed we had no choice but to endure it, however unbearable it might be. Perhaps we would be sent to the same camp as Father; then again, perhaps our family would be scattered to the four winds. I looked out the window and saw soldiers in the street below. They were here; they were coming for us.

But these soldiers were not Germans; they were Italians. Hitler had given Mussolini the southeast of France as a little gift. He didn't realize it, but in doing so he gave the few Jews remaining in the area a bigger gift.

The Italians set up headquarters in the center of Nice, and it became clear from the outset that these men were not the monsters the Nazis were. They immediately let the Jewish people reopen the synagogue. A Jewish committee was set up and given the authority to issue identity papers sanctioned by the Italians. Nice became a mecca for Jews from the once unoccupied zone. Those not immediately arrested by the

German occupation troops or the French police streamed into the area and into the open arms of the Italians. Even though they were fascists, the Italians showed absolutely no hatred toward the Jews. We attributed this phenomenon to the fact that the commander of the occupation forces had a Jewish mistress, something he did not keep a secret.

In reality, however, this was not the reason for the Italians' friendliness. The real reason was that the Italian soldiers were human. They realized that the Jewish people had done nothing wrong and were not even fighting anyone, so they refused to obey Mussolini's strict orders to deliver all Jews in their jurisdiction to the Nazis. All over the zone, forced residences were established, most of them in fine hotels in famous tourist areas. Each area was to hold about one thousand Jews. The "inmates" were given food, lodging, and, above all, safety. We felt quite secure in Nice. The French police were forced to recognize the new identification papers and were therefore unable to arrest and deport Jews.

But that hardly meant we were out of danger. The Nazi demands for French labor were getting more and more overpowering. By the beginning of January 1943, the French police were trying to send me off as a laborer, bypassing the Italian authority over me and forty or so other Jews. Mother talked to the Jewish committee members and was advised that the only way out was to surrender to the Italians and ask them to send me to a forced residence.

I walked into the Italian headquarters, told my dilemma to a high-ranking officer, and asked for help. He was somewhat troubled. He told me they had no openings in any of the existing locations. After talking to other officers, he came up with a solution. I was to be arrested by the Italian army and sent to a civilian prisoner of war camp in Sospel, France. From there I would be transferred to a forced residence in a small town near

Rome. This would take only three or four days. After I was settled, Mother would join me. I was elated with the plan.

The next morning I walked into the headquarters and was told to consider myself under arrest. There was no animosity, no brutality. I was loaded into a truck with some others, and we drove into the mountains. It was about a five-hour ride, and it got rather chilly. Nobody knew how to dress. I did not even own winter clothes. It snowed when we got to Sospel. I had not seen snow since Vienna. We were led inside, and the gates closed behind us. We felt nobody could touch us now.

Italian soldiers processed us, and after a few hours we were led into the mess hall. After our first meal in camp, we were taken to our sleeping quarters. The room held fifty people. Cots were lined up, and the beds were made. An officer apologized for the lateness of the meal and wished us a good night. The barracks had once been used by the French army, and the Italians had converted the facilities into a civilian prisoner of war camp. They kept only British and American civilians here. These people were all rich property owners with superb homes on the Cote d'Azure, and they were treated accordingly. Reciprocity had a lot to do with this; Italy expected England and the United States to treat Italian civilians equally well.

The Italian soldiers were outstanding. They made our beds every morning while breakfast was being served. There were two Orthodox Jews in camp who apparently refused to eat the non-kosher camp food. The commander was very concerned. He had a meeting with the two, and they made a deal. A stove was set up outside the mess hall; uncooked food was delivered, and the two prisoners were allowed to prepare their own kosher meals.

When my expected transfer to Italy hadn't occurred after a few days, I became anxious. Whenever I asked about it I was told *"domani"*—tomorrow. Everything was *tomorrow* with our friends. There was no rush, no hustle in their lives. There was a little dog in camp, a cute, friendly dachshund mix; we called him Domani.

A month later, tired of playing cards and doing nothing, I asked the commander to let me work in the kitchen. He was amazed that someone who did not have to work would volunteer to, but he shrugged and assigned me a pair of army shoes. I was thrilled and went to the kitchen very early in the morning. My new bosses welcomed me with open arms. I was given very light tasks to perform—nothing backbreaking. The kitchen people had special meals, so I started to gain weight.

Mother came to visit one Sunday. She brought warm clothes, homemade pastries, and two one-thousand-lira bills. I do not know how she managed to accomplish this. Money was very important in this camp. Though it was not allowed, most people had some. Soldiers sold all kinds of things for a few lira.

I quit the kitchen after a while and started to hang around the infirmary. Two of the male nurses befriended me and taught me to speak Italian, which did not take long because I had a terrific ear for languages. One night they invited me to go on a ride with them. I did not want to leave this place, but they said it would be fun and very profitable. Against my better judgment I went. They had no problem sneaking me out; nobody checked the truck. The destination was a supply area. Their assignment was to bring hospital supplies to camp, but they also stole a lot of items and were very generous with the loot, giving me a lot of goodies. Cigarettes were a much desired commodity, and I had plenty.

I increased my stash by teaming up with one of my co-prisoners, Siegfried Schwarz, to play cards. He was a European bridge champion and had a keen mathematical mind. He remembered every card played and was unbeatable. We played for cigarettes instead of money and wound up with a lot of smokes. Siegfried and I became not only good friends but confidants. Trust was a very precious commodity in wartime; your friend today might easily become your enemy tomorrow. Siegfried and I knew we would never betray each other. As it turned out, our paths ran in close parallel over the next few years.

It became clear that we had been forgotten in this place. Rome seemed farther and farther away, and I gave up on getting there. I could accept this because it was really very good in Sospel. The future was unclear, but being in Italian hands after the end of the war was certainly one of the better prospects. Win or lose, I was going to live. The trick was to stay alive until the fighting stopped, and that was not a sure thing, not even in a seemingly secure camp like ours.

About two months into my confinement, we prisoners were getting ready to go to breakfast one morning when the soldiers told us to stay put because there was trouble at the gate. A force from Germany's Second SS Panzer Division was outside, with heavy armaments—a couple of tanks, cannons, machine guns—pointed at the camp gate. They asked for the Italian commander and demanded that he surrender all Jews immediately. We watched with horror. But then the incredible happened: the Italians pointed their firepower—tanks, bazookas, antiaircraft weapons, cannons—at the Nazis. It was obvious they were not going to give us up without a fight. The SS looked awesome and mighty; the Italian equipment was no match for the German weapons. The standoff lasted thirty minutes or so, though it seemed an eternity. We were about to give ourselves up when the Nazis packed it in and left the premises. Impossibly, the Italians had stood their ground and won.

April came around. I had now been in Sospel for four months. Passover was upon us, and the Jewish people in camp decided to have a seder. With the cooperation of the camp administration, a field kitchen was supplied, and we were able to cook a kosher meal. During the ceremony, the *marechiallo* and his staff entered the room. They took their hats off to show respect, unaware that Jews prayed with their heads covered. The Italians stayed through the festivities, ate with the congregation, and seemed pleased to be of help. They were wonderful people.

Shortly thereafter, I was called into the office and told I was going to be liberated. It seemed Mother was turning wheels again. She had managed to get us both into a fairly new forced residence in St. Martin Vesubie, a small town at the foot of the Maritime Alps. I was handed discharge papers with instructions to be in St. Martin and report to the Italian authorities within two weeks. I was told how sorry everybody was to lose me, but, not being American or British, I really did not belong here and would be much better off where I was going. I was sorry to leave the camp. I knew what I was leaving behind but did not know what I was going into. But I had no choice. Several others came along, including Siegfried Schwarz. He and I took a bus to Nice. I went home and found Mom. Plans had already been drawn up.

We were among one thousand Jews in this forced residence. Our room was in a house owned by a French woman whose husband had died in the war. She was glad to get some money from the Italians for the rentals. After settling into our new domicile, we went to the Italian headquarters, located in the center of the village. We were told that all we had to do was to come here twice a day and sign in. It was that simple. The Italians knew no Jew was going to run away. Mother found acquaintances and was very happy. As long as there was protection from deportation, everybody was happy.

I met a lot of young people my age. Everyone became friends instantly. I got into a circle of kids interested in learning to swing dance and fell in love with a girl named Adele, who was very pretty and shy. We had long talks; after a while she confided in me that she was pregnant. The father was one of our buddies, a tall, handsome German Jew. No wonder this shy girl fell for him.

It was five years into the Holocaust, and I had still not been deported. Quite a feat. I lived from day to day. Tomorrow was not as important as today. My knowledge of the war was, to say the least, very limited. The Allies seemed to be winning the battles and maybe even the war, but only Nazi propaganda reached us daily. A few people had shortwave radios and could receive Radio London, the BBC. The news from there was pretty encouraging; the Nazis were said to be losing on practically all fronts. The bulletins were so contradictory I did not know what to believe.

I enjoyed my security, but part of me wanted to get into this war. I was tired of running scared, running for my life. The Italians were marvelous hosts, but who knew when they'd find it expedient to abandon us—just as Jean Marell had? At some point, I realized, one had to stop fleeing, stop relying on others, and fight for one's own survival. I ached for the chance to do so.

ㅁ ◊ ㅁ

St. Martin became quite a nice Jewish community. Every Sabbath there were services. The *marechiallo* often came and participated. He loved the voice of our cantor, who came to us from Belgium. There was no doubt in my mind that the Italian soldiers were not cooperating with their German masters. Mussolini's strict orders to surrender all Jews in Italy and in Italian-occupied territories to the Nazis were totally ignored. We did not know how long this would last, but every day was a new gift to all of us.

In September rumors started to circulate that Italy was on the verge of quitting the war. Mussolini was arrested, and all our Italian friends were very happy. The fascist regime had fallen. Everybody hoped for better times now. For almost a month, all kinds of stories surfaced. The Americans were occupying Italy, and the Germans were doing nothing to stop them. Finally, Italy signed an armistice with the Allies. General Eisenhower and Marechiallio Badoglio, Mussolini's successor, signed an independent armistice agreement. Italy had broken ranks with the Axis. The war was over—or so the Italians thought.

The Germans did not see it from the same perspective. They rushed to occupy all of the previously Italian-held territories—including our little village. The situation became chaotic. As far as the Italian troops were concerned, the war was finally over, and they prepared to leave the valley. The Jews did not know which way to turn. Staying in St. Martin without our Italian benefactors would be suicidal. When word arrived that the Germans had already begun to enter the valley leading to St. Martin, the Italian soldiers decided to leave on foot. They parked their trucks neatly in the center of town, packed only what they could carry, and prepared to go into the woods leading to the Alps. Seven hundred of the one thousand Jews in the forced residence decided to follow them into Italy.

I talked to Mother and told her what lay ahead. She dressed accordingly. I opened Dad's trunk and tried on a few of his warmer suits. A green one seemed to fit. We took off. The three hundred or so who stayed behind were mostly women with infants or children, old people with crippling diseases, and those few who had simply given up. Some thought our adventure was doomed; nobody knew where we were going or how to get there. The Italians went ahead and soon lost us.

Fortunately, the mountain path was well marked. Halfway through the trip I was elected to lead the pack; I spoke Italian fluently by now, and we expected to be in Italy soon. Another day and night went by. We were tired and discouraged, desperately lost in the mountains. It was cold; we had passed the treeline long before, and the terrain had become rougher and rougher. Finally we reached a steep incline of about two hundred feet. We had to climb on our hands and knees. When we reached the apex, we were looking into Italy.

We crossed the border, and to my utmost amazement all of my followers had made it. There were cheers and joy all around. We expected to encounter American soldiers at any moment. A short walk ahead we found an Italian fortress, which had probably been built to defend Italy against France during World War I. An Italian lieutenant came out, looked at our group, and wanted to know who we were. I explained that we were Jewish refugees fleeing from the Nazis. I told him we had come a long way and needed help. The officer asked us to follow him into the fortress. It was an armory with barracks for a large number of troops. The commander of the fort gave orders. Soon the kitchen became busy, and cots were set up for us to sleep on. It was a continuation of Italian hospitality toward Jews.

The commander invited me to his office. He wanted to make some calls to his headquarters in Cuneo, the first city on the plain. The captain called his superiors and explained the situation. I heard him say he had seven hundred *Hebrei* on his hands, and he wanted to know how to proceed. We were hoping to be taken by truck to Cuneo and to put the Nazi terror behind us. The captain was put on hold, seemingly forever. When he was reconnected, it was to a different office. The captain was now talking to an officer of the SS. He was ordered to stay put and told that his "problem" would be taken care of with expediency. My stomach cramped up, but I did not panic.

We were awakened about four the following morning by a bugle and told to get our things together. The Italian commander told us to flee, gave us directions toward Cuneo, and advised us to stay away from the main road. We descended into the Valle Gessa. It was a pleasant stroll, but I reminded everybody that we were not free, that Germans were down the road and that we must proceed with utmost caution. Nobody wanted to listen to me. I was called the eternal pessimist.

That afternoon we arrived at Valdieri, a small village with a water fountain and two grocery stores. Everyone bought salami and white bread and settled down to rest. This concentration of noisy Jews made me very uneasy. I knew the Germans were not far away. I found the city hall and talked to the mayor, who consented to issue fake identity cards to whoever wanted or needed them. Mother and I got the first two. Ten of our friends—including the Gorges girl and her parents, Siegfried Schwarz, the Habermans, and Mrs. Sperling—followed suit. I did not know how good these cards would be or whether they would hold up at all, but I urged everybody to take one. But most of the refugees were tired of running and wanted to believe we had reached safety. The twelve of us with identity cards decided to separate from the main group. We went into the woods a bit. It had been almost twenty-four hours since the Nazis had learned about us. If anything was going to happen, it would be soon.

And happen it did. Around four in the afternoon, a motor column of the Wehrmacht entered the village. German soldiers surrounded the little town, set up machine-gun positions, and started screaming in German through their loudspeakers that all the *saujuden* were to surrender immediately. They would not tolerate any resistance; anyone who did not obey these orders would be shot on the spot. These were the Nazis I remembered—arrogant and brutal.

Our friends marched into the trucks without saying a single word. All we could hear was screaming and swearing: *jude, jude, jude,* and more *jude.* When everyone was loaded, the convoy left. Only we twelve remained free.

□ ◊ □

We left the valley immediately. We were told that the next valley to the north, the Valle Stura, was much larger and, as far as anybody knew, was not occupied by the Nazis. We went up a little way, reached the crest of the hill, and came down into a wide plain. I stopped at a tiny store on the side of the path to ask some questions. The shopkeeper told me the Germans patrolled the main road only occasionally. He said to watch out crossing the river, the road, and the railroad track. He gave me four packs of cigarettes, and on we went.

We got to the other side and climbed up a pathway, where a few farmers greeted us cordially. One of them led us into his home, and his wife brought some food. After I had explained our dilemma, they gave us shelter for the night—an empty barn. The farmer was a poor man. He might have had cows and pigs in this barn at one time, I thought; now he had twelve Jews. He told me we could stay here as long as we wanted and refused to take money from us, even though he knew that if the Nazis caught him they would execute him on the spot. All twelve of us were happy to have a roof over our heads. We lay down in the hay and slept deeply.

Next morning the farmer explained the layout of the valley. It had two roads—one main highway and a smaller one used for military traffic. The River Stura flowed through the center of the valley. A small railroad went from Demonte, a village a short distance away, all the way through the valley to the big city of Cuneo. The tiny village we were in was called Moiola. Lots of Italian soldiers who had deserted were here. Some told me that if they had stayed in the army, the Nazis would have taken them to Germany for retraining and eventually sent them to the front against the Allies. They told me Mussolini had been freed by some SS men and was now in Germany.

Eventually I was stopped by a few officers. I told them where we had come from and said the Germans were now on the French-Italian border. These officers, about thirty of them, had deserted their posts and were going into the mountains to await the Allied victory in Italy. He was optimistic that this would not take longer than a few weeks. I became very excited. I was nineteen now, and I wanted to join these men. I wanted to fight back against the Nazis, to stop running. Without hesitation they accepted me into their group.

I told Mom what I was going to do, and she was totally indifferent. I promised I would try to stay in touch; she was satisfied with that. Nobody else from our group wanted to join me. I could understand that; they felt pretty safe where they were.

But safety mattered little to me. My anger had reached the breaking point. The Nazis had chased my family out of Austria, then out of France; they had nearly caught up to me here, in Italy, and they had captured the nearly seven hundred Jewish refugees I was leading and had taken them who knows where. My father had been in their clutches for over a year now. Mother and I had been lucky so far, but sooner or later we were bound to be captured. I was tired of running. I wanted to stop and face the murderers before my time ran out.

5

Biancastella

I was the youngest in my new group, and I felt good about it. We made our way up into the mountains, stopping at a hunter's cabin. The officer in charge told me I was now one of them. He handed me a rifle and said I was now a freedom fighter, a Partisan. This sounded very impressive, and I was very happy. Now I would be able to shoot back. No more would I be chased like an animal. I finally had a chance. I was instructed on how to use my weapon and told that with God's help I would never have to use it. And if God would not help me, then perhaps the weapon would.

I was proud and full of anticipation. We spent the night in the cabin, making a meal of some canned goods and sleeping on straw. The next day we went on, climbing higher and higher into the mountains. We reached a lake and found another cabin, which became our headquarters for a while. One of the men had German hand grenades. When the pin was pulled, the grenade took seven seconds to explode. Our comrade took one, pulled the pin, and threw it into the water. The lake was loaded with trout, and the detonation killed a large number of them. All we had to do was gather them and bring them ashore. We made a fire and had fish for supper. I did not think this way of fishing was legal, but then, war is tough.

For the first time in years I felt really secure. These guys knew what they were doing. I trusted them. But I was still naive, and they weren't above taking advantage of me. One day one of the lieutenants said he wanted to go down into the valley to find out how the war was going. I was the only one in civilian clothes, and he asked me to lend him my suit. It seemed the right thing to do, so I swapped my suit for his uniform and my shoes for his army boots. They fit comfortably, because we were about the same size. He left almost immediately. After several days he still had not returned and was pronounced a deserter. I did not think this was very funny; I was now stuck in an Italian officer's uniform. The guys were all laughing and said that from now on I was a first lieutenant. I had been promoted rather rapidly.

In the inside pocket of the coat I found the officer's identification papers. His name was Enrico Biancastella. He had been born in Bari, in the deep south of Italy, presently under Allied occupation. Therefore, nothing was traceable should we be captured by Nazis. I took this man's name. From now on I was Biancastella—Italian for "white star."

It was only fitting that I should take on a new identity. The life I had known as Heinz Josef Burger was over. I was not going to grow up, take over my father's business, and own season tickets to the Vienna Austria and the opera. The rules had all changed, and if I was going to survive this war I would have to change, too. As Biancastella I immediately became a different person from the one I had been before. I became a resistance fighter.

◻ ◇ ◻

After some time a few of the fellows left us, and some new ones came to join us. One newcomer was Lieutenant Spada. He had only one thing on his mind: killing Nazis. Spada had been imprisoned for treason and assorted other offenses prior to the fall of the fascist government and was released from jail after Mussolini's arrest. Now we had him, and he adopted me. He liked the idea that a Jew—especially a foreign Jew—was so

eager to fight this brutal enemy of Italy. He made me his partner; I had no choice in the matter. Spada declared himself a
colonel so he could have authority over me.

Our small group of Partisans became the nucleus of a
much larger group. Scores of deserters and civilians came into
the mountains to join the fight against the Nazis. It was decided
that all titles would be dropped and that every man would be
called *partigiano*. There were no salutes, and everybody was
considered of equal rank. We called ourselves the First Alpine
Division and sought recognition by the Allies, which did not
come right away.

The winter of 1943 was approaching rapidly. We found
old farm buildings in the hills and mountains and dug in. The
Nazis and fascist troops were not likely to attack us in the
snow. The Germans all but disappeared from the Valle Stura.
I had never been so cold in my life. All I could think about was
summer. Sanitary conditions were poor, to say the least. I
refused to wash with snow or ice water. I always said that
nobody ever died from filth, and we became outstanding
examples of this theory.

I found an old pair of skis and used some old wire to
make improvised bindings. My boots were full of holes, and
the skis were far from professional quality, but I was amazed at
how well I could get around. Three other Partisans also had
jerry-rigged skis, and we decided to go to neighboring farms in
search of food. But the farmers closest to us were as hungry as
we were. We moved on until we found a prosperous-looking
farm—our pot of gold! The farmer was immediately on the
defensive. "No food here," he said. "We have nothing; the
Germans took it all, and my family is starving. I don't know
how we are going to make it through the winter."

I felt sorry for him. If I had had anything to eat, I would
have given it to him. But my friends seemed to know something I didn't. They pressured the old man, threatened him

with everything short of death. His wife came out and cried and pleaded with us. We demanded to see the rest of the farm. We came into a chamber that was quite dark. It was stocked with aged Italian cheese, enough to feed the whole division. The farmer begged us not to take any. He said we would not like it because it was not aged enough. I said, "Let's be nice to him. Let's take only two wheels." It was agreed. We had no money, so I wrote the farmer an IOU so he could get paid after the war was over. He said nothing. He was glad to see us leave.

We took our prize back to our base. Spada grabbed one cheese and proceeded to cut it open while the rest of us looked on. What we saw was disgusting: this cheese was full of little worms. I stood back in horror, but some fellows' faces lit up with joy. They started to eat this mess and loved it. They explained to me that this was a very rare kind of cheese, a specialty that was worth a fortune. I told them I would rather be naked for the remainder of the war than eat worms. A few of us stayed hungry.

After a short while, it was decided that we might as well move closer to Demonte. The total absence of German troops allowed us to take this calculated risk. Life became more tolerable. I thought about my father and the other prisoners in Nazi Germany and wondered how they were surviving the German winter. There was no cause for complaint among the Partisans. If anyone did not like it, he was free to leave. The main reason for our durability was that we were living as free men.

I was able to see my mother a few times. She was tucked safely in the same barn we had found when we first arrived in the Valle Stura. She was glad to see me. It had become quite clear by now that the war was not going to be over quickly. We received information about the slow progress of the Allied armies in the south. I was burning for some action. Except for small raids on enemy depots in attempts to steal weapons and ammunition, we still had done very little to earn the name *Partisan*.

In early spring a German Jew named Walter Marx joined us in the valley. He had been among the group of seven hundred or so refugees arrested in Valdieri on our flight from St. Martin. From him I was able to learn what had become of those unlucky Jews. When the prisoners reached Cuneo, the Nazis surrendered them to the Italians. They were put into an armory, given good food and accommodations, and even allowed to go to town to shop or take in a movie. They felt sorry for the twelve of us who had decided not to follow them. These pleasant circumstances lasted approximately two months. Then one morning a motor column of SS arrived, entered the barracks, and replaced the Italian guards. The Jews were told that the soft life was over. The beatings started instantly. There was a lot of blood. The prisoners were chased to the railroad tracks and loaded into cattle cars. Walter was squashed against the wall of the

22. As a member of the Partisans, spring 1944. Near Demonte, Valle Stura, in the Provincia di Cuneo, Italy.

building by a tank and left for dead. When everybody had gone, he was picked up by some Italian soldiers and transported to an army hospital, where he was nursed back to health. He joined us because he knew it was the only way to stay alive. He had no idea where the train took all the Jews; he knew only that they were deported. Rumors flew that they were taken to a labor camp somewhere in Poland.

As soon as the snow melted, the First Alpine Division fell under German attack. They came up the valley and started into the hills. We were waiting for them. I realized immediately that it took only one of us to take care of a lot of them. We saw them coming, but they had no idea where we were. The battle was short. They lost a large number of men and retreated as fast as they came. I do not recall any losses on our side.

I always wondered if, when the time came, I would be able to pull the trigger and actually shoot another human being. I had not been raised to be a killer. But all I saw in front of me were Nazis—professionally trained Jew killers. I remembered the brutality, the murder; I thought of the Jewish victims, defenseless and unable to fight back. I thought of my father, handcuffed, being shipped off to a concentration camp; I remembered the seven hundred refugees captured before my eyes in Valdieri. And I became their vindicator, an avenger for all the innocent victims the Nazis had terrorized. My adrenalin went into high gear. The enemy was Nazi, and Nazis were inhuman. That's all I needed to know. Did I kill? Yes, I killed.

After this initial engagement, the Germans did not bother us too much. We were able to occupy the valley almost to Borgo San Dalmazzo, where the valley became much wider and it was impossible for us to set up a logical defense. Spada and I set up shop in Demonte. We were important people now. We had sent the Nazis packing and were considered "liberators." If the Germans attacked, we would be alerted in plenty of time to retreat into the mountains to fight them there. In the meantime, we performed a multitude of sabotage acts against the Nazis, who seemingly wanted to ignore us. Undisturbed, we ruled the valley.

The division grew to about twenty thousand men. We discarded our uniforms and got into civilian clothes because, as usual, the Nazis had broken their word. At the start of the Partisan movement, they had dropped leaflets announcing that any fighter taken prisoner in uniform would become a prisoner of war and be treated with respect, in accordance with the Geneva Convention. The first few Partisans captured by the Nazis were tortured to death and thrown back to the place where they had been captured. We caught on rather rapidly.

Not all our men could find civilian clothes to replace their uniforms, but we did the best we could. I received a pair of pants, one shirt, one scarf, and a pair of shoes. I still owned

23. Picture taken in Moiola, Italy, in front of barn Italian farmers provided for Jewish refugees, October 1943. People in top row are, from left, a farmer; a Jewish refugee lady; Seigfried Schwarz (who was executed by the Brigate Nere on the last day of the war); the refugee lady's husband; and another refugee, who was later shot by a Nazi patrol. My mother is the lady seated at left in the center row.

three pairs of socks. I was set for spring and well into summer. Somehow I landed a tommy gun, a semiautomatic weapon. I recalled having seen them before. Almost all American gangster movies featured those weapons. It was quite a cannon. I also had a few German hand grenades and a pistol. I was as safe as one could be in those circumstances.

Mother was moved from her barn to a small room next to the railroad station in Demonte. The Partisans even provided food for her. She took it all in stride; I had the impression that she did not know what was going on. She was just waiting for the war to end.

We had only one more attack during that spring. It was launched by the Italian Brigate Nere, the black brigades, freshly trained fascist troops. They fared no better than their German masters had. They had stopped just before getting to Demonte. We stayed out of sight; they probably thought we had run away. They decided to take a swim in the river; all their clothes came off, and they jumped into the water and had a good time. We swarmed out of the bushes and shot the hell out of them. The survivors reached their trucks and took off without uniforms or guns. The thought of these troops arriving in Cuneo nude and unarmed struck me as funny. That was the first and last attempt by Italian fascists to enter our stronghold.

By now I had become somewhat hardened to suffering and death. I was determined to keep the Nazis away from me, even if it meant killing; it was kill or be killed. But my regard for human life had not disappeared altogether. When two young Partisans about my age were caught stealing small amounts of money from a local grocery store and condemned to be shot by a firing squad, I called for a conference of the military police. To take two young lives for such a small offense was not only unjust but also criminal, I argued; if we shot them, we would be just as bad as the Nazis. They rejected my objections, and to make it even worse they placed me on the twelve-man murdering squad. I was horrified.

This was a public event; the natives were invited to watch. The two boys were brought out, blindfolded, and tied to a stake. They cried and begged for their lives. We had to line up and load our weapons. I had already made up my mind that I was not going to aim at the kids. My bullet was going to go over their heads. The order was given. The shots rang out, and the boys slumped to the ground. They were cut loose. General Rosa approached and gave each of them the coup de grâce—one shot in the head. I thought this was murder. I walked away totally destroyed. Spada congratulated me for being such a good soldier. I told him to shove it. I went up to Rosa, a little, ignorant ex-fascist, and told him what I thought of him and that I would never speak to him again. He was not rattled. He just did not care.

□ ◇ □

The Allied advance was moving at a snaillike pace. Monte Cassino was a tremendous obstacle. The monastery was heavily armed and well defended. Finally, the Americans bombarded it with everything available; they suffered great losses, but they finally captured Monte Cassino. Once this obstacle was removed, the road to Rome was opened.

The news from Radio London was better now. Finally, progress was being made. We began receiving airdrops. We had to listen to the BBC's personal messages prior to the newscasts. If we heard three of our messages in a row, we were on for that night. The first drop was almost on target. It consisted mostly of Vat 69, a very bad whiskey, and Victory cigarettes, which were also bad. Nobody had any complaints. The next drop brought more important items, such as Sten guns, British uniforms, and, especially welcome, a bunch of Eisenhower jackets. The Sten gun drop was almost a disaster. The British wanted to be overly efficient, and they had loaded the guns with the clips in place. On impact, all hell broke loose. The guns started firing automatically. This was the biggest scare of the war for me to this point. Fortunately, nobody got hurt.

Throughout the valleys occupied by our men, the Wehrmacht executed periodic raids. The Valle Stura was usually the least affected. Only once in spring 1944 did they come in force. We were warned quite some time in advance. Mother and the other Jewish refugees were moved to a mountain hut, far from the roads and areas of possible Nazi infiltration. Mom did not want to give up her room, but as usual she followed her orders. The onslaught was unbelievable. Most of us had never seen the German war machine in action. We had no way to defend ourselves. The transplanted Africacorps—soldiers in shorts and armed to the teeth—were leading the attack. Tanks, armored cars, and men rushed into the valley, forcing us into a rather speedy retreat up the mountain. German stormtroopers followed us as if they knew the terrain better than we did. It was scary, to say the least. Soon we just ran; nobody had time to shoot.

We arrived on the crest of a small mountain separating the Valle Stura from the Valle Grana. It started to get dark. Fortunately, the Nazis decided to call it a day. Exhausted, I lay down on the ground. It was pouring rain, but I did not care. We all fell asleep. At dawn we were awakened by a deafening roar. I looked up to see strange aircraft hugging the ridge and plunging into the valley below. The bottom sides of the planes were so close I was certain they saw us and were going to shoot us. I had never seen terror so close that I was almost able to touch it. There must have been a dozen planes. They descended into the valley, and sirens went off; almost immediately we heard explosions beneath. The planes were Stukas, the infamous

German dive-bombers so notorious during the Polish campaign and subsequently in France.

While the battle raged in Demonte, we managed to cross the valley. We were going to wait in the woods adjacent to the main road. It was not long before we heard an awful roar. We took cover in the woods. The road became very busy. Tiger tanks started to patrol the area. These were really big machines, comparable to Sherman tanks, their U.S. counterparts. Their machine-gunners were ready to fire on anything that moved. Nobody dared even to breathe. This went on for the rest of the day. I thought I had been scared before, but I did not know what scared was until this day.

By evening the tank patrols had stopped. We got up hungry, dirty, and jubilant to be alive. The next morning we were able to reoccupy Demonte. What we found was comical. The only damage to this little town had been inflicted on the armory. The Stukas had dive-bombed their own side's positions! Multitudes of Germans had been killed by friendly fire. Their signals had been mixed up somehow, and the whole thing had gone sour. We all escaped without a scratch.

◻ ◊ ◻

My mother was told to stay put. Summer 1944 was fast approaching, and rumors abounded about an Allied invasion of France. We were very hopeful but leery because of all the Germans stationed all over Italy. We had them all: Wehrmacht, Africacorps, Waffen SS, Volkssturm, even Hitlerjugend.

We took a few Germans prisoner on one of our raids and brought them to Demonte to interrogate them. We hoped to find out what their plans were for the near future. I was the interrogator, since I spoke German. One of the prisoners, a young, good-looking Nazi, was terribly afraid we would kill him. I assured him that if he behaved himself, no harm would befall him. A very pretty girl who worked at the restaurant in Demonte was attracted to this Nazi. She wanted to sleep with him, and I wanted to sleep with her. We made a deal: if I did not kill him and we let him go, she would sleep with me instead.

I pulled some strings, and that night we went to raid a gasoline depot near Cuneo. The Nazi came along and was let go after completion of the mission. I could hardly wait to get back. It was very late, almost two in the morning. I found the girl's room, which she shared with an old chambermaid. The lights were left on. The girl was half asleep, but I was not going to be denied because of such a small detail. I dropped my pants and got into bed. The old woman was watching with wide-open eyes. My partner opened her eyes just long enough to ask me if I had done something stupid. She was back in dreamland without realizing what had happened.

On June 6, 1944, we got the news that the Allies had landed at Normandy. Radio London deplored the many losses but called the landings a huge success. The Germans concentrated large numbers of troops at the base of every valley that had a road leading into France. The Valle Stura was one of them.

Later that month, the massive attack into the Valle Stura began. It was a slow process for the German troops. We booby-trapped both roads and blew up all the small bridges over the river. We fought them at each bridge, and the battles always seemed to follow the same script. The Nazis would send two motorcycles first. They'd stop when they saw that the bridge had been blown, and then we would pulverize them. Within a few hours, we would be visited by two trucks, each carrying twenty men and a small cannon. We would attack and destroy them without any difficulty. In another four hours or so, usually two tanks would arrive with soldiers walking behind them. By then we were gone, waiting by the next bridge.

In this way we were able to slow the Nazi advance, but we could not stop them altogether. We finally ran out of bridges, and they were able to pour lots of men into the upper valley—past Vinadio, Pontebernardo, and finally Bersezio. We had no choice but to return to the mountains. It was cold up there, and we were starving. We found a dead cow that had been blown up. Someone took out a hunting knife and cut into the cadaver and started to eat the raw meat. We all did the same. It was food, and nobody worried about dying from it.

The final push came high up near the French border. The assault was made by the Africacorps tanks, but they kept sliding back faster than they could advance. That terrain did not lend itself to tanks in battle. By the time they finally occupied the border, the Americans were waiting for them on the French side. Unknown to us, the Allies had made a secondary landing in the southeast of France and had encountered very little opposition. We had done our job. No German soldier ever crossed the French-Italian border.

High in the mountains, the Partisans held a meeting. We were given a choice. We could cross the border and join the Americans, or we could stay in Italy and wait to be reorganized—if we could stay out of Nazi hands. Walter Marx and I had our own powwow. I had my mother to consider. If I went to France, she would never have known what happened to me, and I would be unable to make sure she was safe. I decided to return to the Valle Stura, and Walter agreed to join me.

We took our time making our descent, foraging for food along the way. We found lots of berries, but most were rotten. At one point we saw two men at a distance below us. Walter thought they were Germans, but I did not think so. I told him I would go ahead and check it out; when the coast was clear, I would give him a sign. I came very close to the two men, who were picking berries. They were German soldiers. It was too late to run; the only thing I could do was greet them. They wanted to know what I was doing there, and in Italian I told them I had been a prisoner of the Partisans and that the good Germans had liberated me. I told them I was very ill and that I needed medical attention. They bought my story; they probably did not understand half of what I said. In very bad Italian, they advised me to go into the valley and said the German army would get me to a hospital. I thanked them and walked away.

Walter was watching me from above. As soon as I got far enough away from the Nazis, I made a run for it. I made a sign with both hands to warn Walter. He thought I was giving him the all-clear. He came toward the soldiers, recognized that they were Germans, and started to run. I only heard *"Halt, Hände hoch."* Walter kept running. I heard a few gunshots, and then everything was quiet again. An out-of-breath Walter joined me down below, untouched by German bullets. He gave me hell.

Luckily, we encountered no other Germans. As we approached Mom's refuge, a peasant offered us a few small boiled potatoes. We gratefully accepted and ate them right away. We had eaten almost nothing for seven days. Walter and I arrived at Mother's refuge and were welcomed with open arms. She thought I had been killed during the last German offensive.

While we were there, the Italian fascists dropped leaflets from small planes. They urged all defeated Partisans to come to Cuneo, surrender to the Italian authorities, and join the new fascist army. They promised total amnesty. Everybody would be forgiven, and no questions would be asked. Walter and I thought it seemed like a good opportunity to come out of hiding for a couple of weeks and regain our strength. We decided to go for it, totally disregarding the fact that we were Jews, that if we had simply been seen taking a shower we could have gotten ourselves killed.

We took the little train to Cuneo. Before doing anything I went to visit two women I knew, a mother and daughter, who were ironclad Partisan supporters. They had the whole story on the amnesty, and they let Walter and me stay with them. There were so many Partisans in town that it looked like we had occupied Cuneo. The lines for signing up were extremely long. Walter and I waited all day, then were told to come back the next day. We finally reached the front of the line. Our "induction" was a monumental joke. All they did was ask my name, date of birth, and, if I wanted to tell, my place of birth, although this was not a must. They put this information into a large ledger, made me sign, and just like that I was in the army. An identification paper was issued to protect me from Nazis and Italian fascists. Now I was on their side.

So many people volunteered that they were unable to handle the volume. They did not have enough uniforms, weapons, or beds for all the new recruits. My new commanders said anyone who was able to get a room outside the barracks should do so and report back in the morning for assignments. I slept at my friends' house every night and just came in for the meals. It took them about two weeks to catch up.

Then one afternoon as I came in, the doors closed behind me. I was led into a large room to be issued a new uniform. I looked stupid as a soldier of the Italian army. They issued a carbine, making sure none of us had any ammunition to fit it. We were assembled and taken for a walk. They wanted to parade us through town and show us off. Everybody knew who and what we were and found this to be very comical, to say the least.

By now I'd had a couple weeks' respite from the mountains, so my tenure as a member of the fascist army had served its purpose. Now I had to find a way out of my unit before it was shipped off somewhere. I took my civilian clothes to my two female friends' house, and we arranged my desertion. All of us took the train to Borgo San Dalmazzo and got off at the station. There were quite a few Brigate Nere at the depot, watching everybody, but I was never questioned. After all, I was one of them. As soon as the train started up again, I jumped back on. The baffled soldiers were so taken by surprise that nobody even tried to fire a shot at me. In the distance, I saw them talking to my friends, who simply denied knowing me. Nothing happened to them.

As the train moved closer to Demonte, I changed into my civilian clothes, which had been conveniently left on the train. I fled the station, disappeared into the woods, and reached safety. I met some of my comrades, who welcomed me and were surprised that I had the nerve to bring along the carbine. This officially ended my career as a fascist. I was a Partisan again.

□ ◊ □

Shortly after my return to the mountains, one of our leaders met with me and said he had a proposition for me. I could decline if I so chose. It seemed the Catholic Church had been advised that there were Jewish refugees in our part of the world and that they needed everything. The local priests did what they could, but the congregations were small and poor in this mountainous area. The archdiocese in Genoa had collected money to help out. Priests were to distribute food and clothing to the needy Jews. The only drawback was that someone had to go and get those items. Because of my youthful appearance (I still had not grown a beard) and my newly acquired army identification papers, I was asked to go. I told him I might accept this mission, but I did not think the papers from the army would do me any good. If I were stopped in civilian clothes, I would probably be shot as a spy or at least be put in jail for being AWOL.

The *marechiallo* made new documents for me, with a photograph and all. I was supposed to be fifteen years old, and I looked the part. I destroyed the papers I had received from the army. Then I went to tell Mother that I would be gone for a little while and that she should not worry.

Meanwhile, Siegfried Schwarz came up with one of his brilliant ideas. His parents were in Como, a beautiful tourist town on Lake Como. There the Italians had about a thousand Jews under their protection, much as they used to in St. Martin Vesubie. I was surprised to learn about this. I thought such arrangements had ended with the Italian surrender. Since I was going to be in Genoa anyway, said Siegfried, how far could it be to Milan, then to Como? I should go to his folks to investigate the possibility of our being accepted into this area of bliss. I said I would try.

I departed and was not even scared. I do not know why I did all the crazy things I did. I never thought about being arrested once I was into a project. I went to Cuneo, then took a train to Genoa. I even saw the bishop, who praised me for my courage and wished me all the best. He told me they had a program to protect Jewish people and that many had been taken to safety by the church. I was handed a sealed envelope and sent on my way.

I decided I would give Como a shot. It was not a long trip to Milan. In the railroad station in Milan there was an abundance of German army personnel. All were headed in different directions, and none cared who was around them. I think they were already aware they were going to lose the war. I remembered this beautiful railroad station from the time we had vacationed in Stresa before the war.

The trip to Como was just a hop. I found Siegfried's parents, who were settled in a gorgeous area overlooking the lake. They had complete protection from the Nazis. In fact, I cannot recall seeing even one Nazi around there. I was informed that it was impossible to be accepted into this group at the present time and that Siegfried and I should stay where we were. The war was going well, and the Germans were being beaten everywhere. It was all going to be over soon. The Schwarzes packed a small suitcase for their son and presented me with a new pair of boots. I was thrilled. I really needed new boots, because my old pair had long since worn out. The fact that this pair was two sizes too small did not faze me—better squeezed than wet and cold.

Before I left, I took one more look over the mountains. There was Switzerland. How nice it must be there! Then I got on my train and headed back south. The British had finally succeeded in bombing the only railroad bridge over the River Stura, so the passengers had to get off and cross on a temporary hanging walkway. It looked very fragile and was kind of swaying in the breeze, but it was the only way across. The Germans had to use it to get supplies and armament across the river and to their advance positions on the border. I thought this was terrific—anything to make it harder for the Nazis.

I delivered the money to the Catholic relief workers, went ahead to Mother's place, and gave Siegfried his goodies. He was elated. Siegfried was always the dirtiest of the refugees and always wore his only suit, which was made of some camouflage material. His hair was never combed. Now he had new clothes. He washed and even combed his hair. I was not used to his new look. In my opinion, he still looked like one of those caricatured Jews of the Nazi propaganda in the *Sturmer.*

I rejoined the reorganized Partisans, who were stronger and better than ever. With winter approaching rapidly, it was time to get Mother back into her little room in Demonte. The Germans were still in the valley but were not as numerous as they had been a few months ago. Mother settled happily into her winter place. I think she had gotten tired of her mountain life—nothing to do, nowhere to go.

I soon acquired a new friend—a very large, good-humored ex-army mule named Gina. There was a large concentration of Partisans in Valgrana, and we had to transfer a lot of supplies over one mountain and down into the next valley—

extensive climbing and descending. Gina was a back-saver, carrying large amounts of supplies. The mule came with a sidekick, Guido, a native of Venice with a foul temper and a tremendous hatred for the Nazis. He was okay in my book. Once or twice he pulled a gun on me, and I pulled mine on him, which quieted him right down. He was good in the mountains—he was strong and willing to rub Gina down after every trip.

In late fall I checked on Mother once more. I arrived late one night with food for her. We chatted a little, and I decided to stay overnight. Because it was late and an especially dark night, I did not care to be out in the woods alone. I crawled into bed with Mother and fell asleep almost immediately.

I was awakened rather suddenly. Loud knocks at the door in the middle of the night never signified anything good. I opened the door a little and was practically thrown into the room. Two large German soldiers entered and demanded to know my name. They spoke Italian as poorly as my mother did. I pretended I hardly understood them. They said, *"Name und Alter?"* (name and age?). They did not ask for papers, which was strange. They had a clipboard and wrote everything down. Finally, they ordered me to come to the German headquarters at seven the next morning to report for work. They needed men to load and unload the little train where the bridge had been blown.

I was trapped. If it had not been for Mother, I would have disappeared instantly. However, I could not possibly move her by morning. If I did not show up, the Nazis would be back for sure and would discover that Mother was a Jew. I had no choice but to report. But I was not about to break my back all day for these murderers. Upon my arrival at headquarters, I asked to speak to the commanding officer. I told him I had been asked to help load and unload the train. I also told him I spoke perfect German; therefore, I would be useful as an interpreter. It would certainly expedite the work of the "volunteers" and of all Italians if they could understand what was

expected of them. The officer acted as if he had found a gold
mine. He called the two soldiers in charge of this daily chore
and told them to take me along and watch over me. I was here
to help, and they were to treat me like one of their own.

The two soldiers asked why I spoke such good
German. I told them my family had lived in Vienna for a long
time before the war. Dad had a good job there, but we came
back home after the war had started. I was trapped in this god-
forsaken area all by myself and would join my parents in Bari
as soon as the war ended. One of the two soldiers told me he
was from Vienna and was amazed at how well I spoke German.
I told him where I had lived in Vienna and where I had gone
to school. He told me he grew up just a few blocks from where
I had lived and said we could have run into each other with a
little luck. I thought it was lucky we had not met in Vienna; if
he had recognized me, I would probably be dead by now.

We began moving the supplies across the temporary
bridge. In Italian, I told the workers to take their time and not
to strain any muscles or backsides. They understood what I
was trying to do; the work went slowly but perfectly. It took
us most of the day to unload and reload two very tiny freight
cars. Nobody gave the workers a hard time; the Germans
were ignorant and happy. Once in a while a couple of British
fighter planes flew over the area, and the two brave warriors
from the thousand-year Reich seemed very much afraid. I
was right there with them. I did not want to get killed by one
of our allies.

When we returned to their headquarters, the two Nazis
told the commander what a great help I had been. He ordered
the cook to give me a complete dinner—bratwurst, potatoes,
and sauerkraut. Immediately thereafter I went to Mother's
place, took her out of the room, and brought her to the barn
with the other Jews. She would have to spend the remainder of
the winter a little less comfortably.

The next morning I went back for my second day of work. I no longer had to worry about Mother's safety and was ready to get back to the mountains. At the end of the day we took the train back to Demonte. The two Nazis asked me to hold their rifles while they used the bathroom. I took off and ran toward the woods. By the time the Germans were finished, I was only a mirage. Gone was I, and gone were the guns. They yelled and screamed *"Schweinehund, dreckkerl,"* and other German words directed only toward undesirables such as me. I had to laugh as I imagined them explaining to their superiors how they had lost their rifles to a stupid Italian kid.

I met with our guys a little later. They were very amused, but the *marechiallo* called me all kinds of names. He said I had risked my life unnecessarily by going back the second day for two lousy Nazi rifles. We had better weapons anyway. I had to agree with him. I was pleased he cared. That was the last time I left our men to go anywhere. I swore to myself that I would come down from the mountains only to sabotage Nazis or, finally, as a victorious soldier of this war.

I got Gina back, and Guido and I loaded her up again. I did not know where all the supplies were coming from. Guido told me the materials came from Allied airdrops. This might very well be our last trip to Valgrana. We were due to stay there from now on. As we came close to the mountain crest, it started to snow heavily. I said to Guido that I had only seen snow like this in the Alps. As we went on, visibility became zero. I held on to Gina's tail, and Guido held on to me. I hoped Gina knew where she was going. She did; this wonderful animal knew the entire trail to perfection. One slip and we would be buried, not to be found until the snow melted. My face was iced up and frozen. I thought my eyebrows would break up. Finally, late that night, Gina stopped. We had arrived. I saw the familiar barns, and all the friendly people came to unload the mule. Spada came after me and made me rub down my mule before I

was allowed to eat supper. He told me Gina was more important than any of us. He was right. Gina could carry as many supplies as a handful of men. We were all workhorses, and she
worked harder than any of us.

□ ◊ □

The spring of 1945 approached, and we made preparations for
an offensive. Finally, we were going to push back the German
invaders. I knew the war was coming to an end, and if I could
manage to stay alive just a little longer, I would be able to
resume a normal life.

My hygiene was deplorable. I had a bad case of scabies,
a very contagious skin disease brought on by filth and the
numerous varieties of lice we had collected over the many
months spent in barns and the woods. Head lice were rather
easy to take care of; one simply shaved one's head. Body lice
were more difficult to get rid of. Only a good bath and new
clothes could solve that problem, and these were luxuries we
could scarcely afford. I owned three pairs of socks and wore
them all at the same time. Once a week I rotated the outer one
to the inside and so on. Everything was unspeakably dirty. I got
used to it. Eventually I was able to get a hot bath. Spada somehow procured a tube of sulfur cream, the only medicine capa-
ble of helping my skin condition. It was very painful, but the
condition did improve. Nevertheless, I still had my contami-
nated old clothes. I was promised new clothing as soon as
spring came.

Airdrops were coming, and I was first in line for a new
uniform. But all we received were weapons. I tried a Fiat
semiautomatic, but it shot too fast, jammed frequently, and
used too much ammunition. I preferred my trusty Sten gun. I
had to be within ten feet of my target to hit it, but the gun
never failed me.

I used aluminum Italian hand grenades as detonators for the new explosives dropped by the Allies. These were plastic explosives that came in one-kilo tubes and were very dangerous. We were advised never to cut the tube with anything metal. I used a flat piece of wood to carve out just enough space to fit the little grenade into it and then secured it with some string. This was a formidable bomb, able to destroy truckloads of Nazis. One was usually enough.

Spring was almost upon us, and the snow was melting rapidly. We started to get busy. Orders came from the Allied headquarters: we were to sabotage all electrical power plants. All of the railroads in northern Italy were electrified by now. By cutting the power, we could stop the trains; no trains, no supplies; no supplies, no war. Trucks were traveling only at night, and they were to be attacked and destroyed. Every vehicle, from baby carriages to fire engines, was to be taken off the road. I did not quite understand that order, but later it became crystal clear.

One of the most important orders was to rescue U.S. pilots who were forced to parachute after their planes were hit. The United States conducted carpet bombings of industrial cities in the north of Italy. Almost daily, more than a thousand flying fortresses soared overhead in the direction of Milan and Torino. This was an awesome sight. It became so dark that it looked as if night had arrived early. After the mission was completed, some returning aircraft were often too heavily damaged to make it back to France. The crews had orders to try to parachute over Partisan-occupied territories. We could then pick them up, take care of them, and get them back to France, where they were reoutfitted and made ready to fly again. As far as I was concerned, this was one of our most important jobs during the war. No American was allowed to fall into Nazi hands.

When President Roosevelt died in early 1945, we were devastated. We did not understand how a democratic country functioned. Everybody thought that with the change of leadership we might have to face a new U.S. policy of involvement. Nobody knew what Harry Truman was all about. We thought he might pull the United States out of the war.

We became reassured almost right away. About two hundred paratroopers of the 101st Airborne Division were dropped in our zone. They told us they had come to fight and to teach us how to handle this brutal enemy. None had ever seen a Nazi. They all seemed very tough. Hanging around these guys, I started to learn the English language. It came very easily to me. I did not know that the English I was hearing was a little rough; I picked it all up, dirty language or clean.

About this time Spada and I decided to pay a visit to some of our wounded boys, who were kept in a makeshift hospital in Valgrana. On the side of the mountain were a few old empty barns. Cots had been set up, and the Partisans who were hit in battle and did not die were brought here and treated as well as possible. Drugs were unavailable, and the few doctors available had no instruments with which to operate. Usually, gangrene set in after a while, and the patients died. But now things got a bit better. Allied airdrops brought us medication and bandage material. Operating room instruments were provided, and disinfecting materials were available.

As we entered the room, we were hit by an unbelievable stench. To this day it is still in my nostrils. The boys might have been disinfected, but the room certainly was not. This was before the age of penicillin or antibiotics; healing was slow and sometimes not possible. We left thankful that we had never caught a bullet and hoping we never would.

Spada and I rejoined our men. On the way we remarked upon the total absence of cats, which had once been plentiful in the area. Laughingly, I said to Spada that too many "chicken" meals had been eaten lately. Because we had so many men and so little food, cats made a good substitute for chicken. They were also much easier to catch. They really tasted like chicken. Occasionally, when our boys tried to entertain the local women, they served this "chicken," and on a separate platter they brought the chopped-off heads of the pussycats. After the screaming stopped, the women had no appetites, and the boys had more food for themselves. Unfortunately, the absence of cats gave the rodents free reign. Some field rats looked like cats; if the war did not end soon, they would be next on the menu.

The air deliveries came fast and furious. Bazookas, anti-aircraft guns, and assorted light artillery pieces were dropped. Bazookas and plastic explosives were particularly welcome and useful to our way of fighting. We inflicted such heavy losses on the Nazis that they decided to pull back and take refuge in the cities. They never knew what to expect from us. After they evacuated the Valle Stura, we immediately established head-quarters in Demonte. It was like the good old times again. More and more Italian deserters came to join our ranks. Nobody was turned back. Everybody wanted to beat the Germans.

24. In Borgo San Dalmazzo, Valle Stura, just before the Nazi defeat in Italy, April 1945.

Mother came back to town, and I hoped she could stay this time. She gave me very bad news. Haberman, one of the twelve Jews who had escaped from France with us, had strayed too far and was stopped by a German patrol. He ran and was shot in the back, killed. Siegfried Schwarz had been caught by a group of Brigate Nere and taken to Cuneo. I hoped the fascists were kinder than the Nazis and would not execute him.

Our nightly attacks on German positions became more and more powerful. One night stands out in my mind above all others. At about four in the afternoon we received orders to raid an electrical power plant located close to a railroad depot in the vicinity of Valgrana. The Nazis used trains to transport supplies and, occasionally, troops. We were to blow up the tall metal towers that supported the high-voltage wires.

We came out of the valley just as it got dark, found a barn, and went to sleep. At about three in the morning we reached the poles and prepared them for destruction. We used plastic explosives with acid-filled detonators. An hour delay was ample time to allow us to get into position. We usually took our place in the ditches beside the road. After a blast, Nazi troops always came to investigate and possibly to catch a bunch of Partisans. We had to wait for the fireworks.

Immediately after the explosion, we saw flares go up all around the area and heard trucks approaching. The Nazis responded, and we were ready for them. We had a wire stretched across the road that was connected to a large amount of explosives. This booby trap was intended to stop the convoy. We waited calmly.

The noise became louder, and all of a sudden they were upon us. They had come in force. I was ready, a plastic home-made bomb in hand. The lead truck hit the wire and blew up. We threw our bombs onto the rest of the trucks. All of them blew. After the noise died down, only cries of pain and distress could be heard. Some of the injured Nazis had managed to send up flares. The roadside lit up like daylight. The devastation was enormous—tangled metal and dead Nazis all over the place. I felt no emotion. Life meant nothing—especially German life.

We had to get out in a hurry; reinforcements were sure to arrive shortly, and we had no more bombs to throw. As we retreated we heard traffic approaching on the road. There were more flares and a lot of shooting. We ran like hell. The Nazis were no more than five minutes behind us, and daylight was already upon us. We made it into our beloved hills. Later we learned we had killed at least 120 Nazis.

Meanwhile, the systematic destruction of trains and supply vehicles continued. We often took German prisoners. We disarmed most and let them go because we had no place to put them, but we kept the most important individuals to interrogate them. Because I spoke German, I was the principal interviewer. Walter might also have served in this capacity, but he had disappeared, and nobody knew where he was. I hoped he had gone to France and was not captured again. In France the war was over, and he should have been free.

One day a trainload of Nazis arrived. The top-ranking officer was an *obersturmbandführer* of the Totenkopf SS. He was detestable, a trained Jew-killer. In my interview with him, he expressed the view that Hitler should exterminate all the Jews in the world. Up to that point, I believed that captured Jews were kept alive and made to work in German factories; I believed they would return after the war was over. This man told me that most Jews were already dead and that the rest would soon follow them. I became outraged, but he stood before me defiantly. I took him outside behind a tree and told him I was a Jew and that I was going to shoot his stupid Nazi ass off. He tried to run, but he didn't get far; I killed him. Nobody questioned me.

I was disgusted with the war by now. What kind of world was this? One man delighted in killing Jews; another found satisfaction in killing Nazis. People lived amid hunger, filth, disease, and violence; they lived like animals. How different from the world I had grown up in, with its petty comforts and concerns. My old Hebrew teacher, Rabbi Frankfurter, who once seemed so fearsome and omnipotent—how had he fared in this world? What of the soccer players I once worshipped? What of my father's thirty impeccably tailored suits, a different one for each day of the month? They meant nothing; it was as if they had never existed. Father wore prison flannels now, if he lived at all. As for me, I wore the same foul clothes day after day—slept in them, fought in them, killed in them. How I longed to change out of them.

With the war finally coming to an end, I decided to get myself deloused—a good, hot shower and some disinfectant did the trick. My clothes were burned, and I watched with great pleasure. Spada brought me a brand-new uniform of the 101st Airborne. He told me we had been honored by the Americans and were authorized to wear this uniform. The only difference was that we wore armbands to identify us as Partisans. I was very proud. I knew I belonged, that I was one of the good guys.

Around the end of April we came down from the mountains. An enormous number of Partisans in green uniforms filled the valley. I recall a very large area in the plains close to Borgo San Dalmazzo where farmers' wives were boiling water in enormous kettles over open fires. They were helping our boys dye their uniforms. It was important to wear a different color than the enemy. I said goodbye to Gina. She was allowed to graze freely now; her work was finished. One of the more helpful farmers would take care of her; she got a well-deserved home, and I was happy for her. I hoped I would never again have to ride another mule.

The final destruction of a ruthless enemy was close at hand. On May 1, 1945, we hit the roads. All of a sudden we had cars and trucks and all sorts of motor vehicles. I did not know where they all came from. Spada picked me up in a Lancia Fuori Seria. It was a luxury convertible, probably abandoned by a high-ranking Nazi. I got in, and we drove in the direction of Cuneo. It was night, and nobody else was on the road. We got to the city limits and still did not encounter any resistance. I was riding shotgun; I had a British bren gun on top of the windshield. Guido was the driver, and he drove very fast.

At dawn I looked around and saw Italian and American flags hanging everywhere. It was amazing. There were no Nazis anywhere. We continued toward the bridge over the River Stura. We drove onto the bridge, and Guido sped up again. Suddenly, he made a stop and got out of the car. "Have a look," he said. The center section of the bridge had disappeared. The Nazis had blown it up. It was almost impossible to see it until we came right up to it. Guido had stopped the car about one meter from the missing link. I would have resented dying like that.

The sun rose, and the city came to life. People came out of their homes to cheer and greet us. We were the liberators they had been awaiting for so long. The Nazis had left in a hurry and on foot; they were afraid to surrender to the Partisans, assuming we were like them, brutes who would torture prisoners to death.

Germany capitulated to Italy on May 2, 1945. The war was over. The German army marched toward Milan, badly defeated and in rags but as monstrous as ever. On their way to a prisoner of war camp they conducted one last campaign of savagery and terror. Every farmhouse on their way was emptied of all inhabitants, who were lined up against the wall and shot. The houses were then set afire. Only the smallest child was allowed to live. When the troops arrived in Milan, they were received by the Allies and interned with no questions asked. I still cannot understand what prompted these men, knowing the war was not only over but had been lost, to continue their brutal killings. The teachings of the Nazis must have been very thorough. I was devastated to hear the horror stories told by the Italian people.

More devastation awaited me at the prison in Cuneo. I found Siegfried Schwarz lying in the courtyard. He had been executed by the Brigate Nere shortly before our arrival. What disappointment, what pain. He was dead and I was still alive, but it could just as easily have been the other way around. There was no explanation for this outcome, no reason for it. This had been a war without reason. Now, thank God, it was over, and I had survived. I, Heinz Josef Burger.

It was two days before my twenty-first birthday.

6

The Return to France: The Waiting Game

On May 8, 1945, Germany unconditionally surrendered. The war was really over. But we had no time for celebrations. Much work lay ahead.

There were many arrests, and Nazi collaborators were put on trial. The tribunal was composed of Partisans from the military police. It was a swift process; every individual was allowed about two minutes to defend him- or herself. Most were found guilty of treason and condemned to die. When thirty people had been sentenced, they were led to the prison wall and shot by machine guns. It was not pretty, but it was necessary. I hoped mistakes were not made. Guilt had to be established by testimony and documentation. We were usually able to pick out the innocent. The trials lasted probably a week. We didn't stop until the jail was empty. Many people died.

In addition to serving on the tribunal, I was given orders to close the local bordello so the ladies could be examined by a doctor. This assignment made me the most hated man in town, but it was a necessary step; we did not want to spread any diseases contracted from the Nazis. When the bordello reopened a week later, the first man in line was a priest in civilian clothes. Well, he was only an army priest.

I went to Borgo San Dalmazzo and found that Mother had already been brought there. She had been given new clothes and looked very thin, but altogether she seemed quite well. I told her I would pick her up as soon as I was discharged, and we would return to Nice.

I went back to Cuneo, where, to my amusement, I came across two old German soldiers walking with a carriage and two horses. They were Volkssturm. They stopped me and asked in their best German where the headquarters were. Amazingly, they thought the war was still being fought. They complained that they had been sitting on the French border and had not received any supplies for quite some time. I told them to follow me, and they did, gratefully—right into prison. Only then did I tell them that their side had lost the war.

When the Americans arrived in Cuneo, they issued an order to all units: every SS captured was to be put to death without trial in retaliation for the Germans' actions in their last offensive in the Ardennes, where they had shot all American prisoners without exception. I loved this order. But there was one problem: most of the SS had escaped into the mountains. We were supposed to chase them and bring them down, and we were not about to do this. We knew how tough it would be to track the enemy in those mountains, having hidden there ourselves. So we waited.

One by one, they came down, and we rounded them up. They were easily recognizable: their blood type was tattooed under their armpit. They'd been marked this way so they could always get immediate help if wounded in battle, but now the marking had turned against them. The captured SS were led to a large field and made to dig their own graves. They had to lie in the holes and were machine-gunned one by one. We kept a few alive to bury the others. We were not about to dirty our hands. I refused to touch any of them.

In June, Spada asked me if I intended to stay in Italy. He had a big job for me as police chief in Borgo San Dalmazzo. I would get Italian citizenship. I told him I wasn't interested; I wanted to go to Nice to see if my dad had survived. He understood and promised that I would be the first man discharged from the unit. The First Alpine Division was probably the

MINISTERO DELL' ASSISTENZA POST-BELLICA

M.G.   COMMISSIONE REGIONALE PIEMONTESE
PER LA QUALIFICA DI PARTIGIANO

Copia del N. 6710

Torino, 11-17/6/46

La COMMISSIONE REGIONALE PIEMONTESE per l'accertamento
delle qualifiche di partigiano combattente, caduto, ferito in azione
partigiana, mutilato o invalido per la lotta di Liberazione, patriota
(D. L. 21-VIII-1945. n. 518)

- Visto il foglio notizie;
- Sentite le testimonianze dei membri delle Formazioni da cui
dipendeva l'interessato;
- Attuati ulteriori accertamenti:

D E L I B E R A

Il Volontario' _____ BUERGER HEINZ
nomi partigiani assunti _____ BIANCASTELLA
figlio di _____ ELIA _____ e di _____ PORICS TERESA
nato a _____ VIENNA _____ (Prov. _____) il _____ 10/5/24
(AUSTRIA)
residenza abituale _____ CUNEO PRES SPADA _____ via _____ CORSO DANTE N° 53
Distretto militare di appartenenza _____ /
ha diritto alla qualifica di _____ PARTIGIANO COMBATTENTE
con il seguente periodo di servizio:

Formazioni cui ha appartenuto   Periodo di appartenenza

I° DIV.G.L. POLIZIA	dal 1/5/44	al 8/6/45
	dal	al
	dal	al
	dal	al

con le funzioni di:

PARTIGIANO	dal 1/5/44	al 8/6/45
	dal	al
	dal	al
	dal	al

IL PRESIDENTE DELLA COMMISSIONE
(Gen. A. Trabucchi)

25. Discharge document from the First Alpine Division.

largest of the divisions, and I was glad I didn't have to wait in
line to get out when the time came.

Exactly one month after the war was over Spada called
me in. As promised, I was the first man discharged. I was given
a small amount of money and told to contact the Americans,
who would transport Mom and me back to France. I surrendered my weapons and felt at least two thousand pounds
lighter. It had been quite some time since I had not had guns
to lug around. I was put on a lead jeep of a U.S. motor column
on its way to Nice. They stopped long enough to pick up my
mother, and we bid Italy goodbye. I was sad to leave this wonderful country and its terrific people, but I was eager to put the
pieces of my life back together.

□ ◊ □

The climb into France was very slow. I had forgotten how high
the border was. Finally, we crossed the Col Madelena into
France. Rapidly, we drove through Barcelonette and made our
descent toward Grasse and finally into Nice. It was dark by
now, and we were taken to a comfortable hotel in the center of
town, the headquarters of the French Liberation Army. Mother
wanted to go home immediately; I had to remind her that we
had no home anymore.

In the morning I was called into a small room, where a
French lieutenant greeted me. He said it felt great that the war
was finally over and that we could all go home soon. I can't go
home, I told him; there's nobody left in Vienna. His ears
perked up. "In Vienna?" he asked. I explained that I was an
Austrian Jew who had spent the war trying not to be killed by
the Nazis. That seemed to concern him. He looked up some
papers and said that because I had been born in Vienna I was
considered a German, and therefore I had to be put into a holding area to be checked out. I told him that was insane; I had

worn the uniform of the 101st Airborne and had just been discharged from the Italian First Alpine Division. "Never heard of it," he replied.

He assured me it would not take them long to verify my story; it was simply a precaution. I told him to check my records at the police station, which would tell him who I was and where I came from. In the meantime, Mother and I would be held at the Hotel Swisse. I remembered the hotel; it overlooked the Mediterranean and was quite classy. How bad could it be? I could use a vacation; life could begin a little later.

We were driven to the hotel. As soon as we entered we were separated. This was no hotel; it was a prison. I was put in a room with twenty or so other guys. There were no beds or furniture, only some hay to sleep on. I was allowed to keep my personal effects, but that was all.

When I found out who my cellmates were, I didn't know whether to laugh or cry. Most were German SS who had escaped from Italy after the end of the war. These were the men we had been ordered to execute, the ones we had missed. Now I was in the same cell with them. What an irony. How thin the distinction was between this war's winners and losers—if there was any distinction at all.

It was humiliating to have to put up with this degradation after all I had been through. Every room was guarded by a French soldier at all times. The food was dished out in the rooms. Nobody was allowed out unless permission was given. The hygiene was deplorable; we all had to share one filthy bathroom. My fellow prisoners didn't seem to mind. They had escaped certain death in Italy and found themselves in a facility they did not think to be so bad. Anti-Semitic talk went on constantly. I did not communicate with any of them. I certainly was not going to admit that I was Jewish; I had no death wish. They all laughed at me, thinking it hilarious to have someone in an American uniform incarcerated with the likes of them. They had not lost any of their audacity. Adolf Hitler and Nazi Germany forever—that was their daily motto.

I desperately tried to find a French officer to lend an ear and get me out of this hellhole. Nobody cared enough to hear me out. I wondered how Mother was taking this terrible episode. Being arrested by Germans was normal, but being arrested by French army personnel? Unacceptable. I was rotting away, and nobody even knew I was there.

After about three weeks of this torture, I got my chance. A French officer of the military police had stopped in front of our room. I jumped out in front of the guard and grabbed him by the arm. In fluent French I begged him to listen to me. The guard was about to pull me away, but the officer waived him off. He took me to his office, where I gave him detailed information about my whereabouts and activities during the war. I told him my records were in the police station in the Rue Gioffredo. I also asked him to get in touch with Monsieur Augier, the attorney who had helped defend Dad when he was arrested in 1942. I was sure Augier would vouch for me and my mother. The officer promised to check it all out. If my story was true, we would be free in a few days.

My hopes were up, but I did not entirely trust the French. I could only stand this misery for so long. I was hungry, and my nerves were frayed from such a long period of close contact with my mortal enemies. But there was nothing I could do except listen to the Nazis tell war stories that were all too familiar to me. If I had had one of my homemade plastic bombs I would have blown up the whole bunch, myself included.

Exactly two days later the lieutenant came to my room and brought my release papers. He said all the information checked out and that he was terribly sorry for what the French army had put me and my mother through. When I got to the main door, Mother was already waiting for me. She was happy to see me. "Let's get the hell out of here," I said. And at last we started to live again.

◻ ◊ ◻

We walked to the Rue de France and picked up a tram. I had a few lira, but they were no good here. The conductor let us ride free.

The tram stopped at the corner where we once had rented the apartment from Madame Perichon. What a strange coincidence! I had not looked at which line we were taking; all I had wanted was to get away from that hotel. Madame Perichon was elated to see us alive. She immediately offered us the apartment we had once occupied. Just take it, she said; we could pay when we could afford it. If we couldn't pay, that would be okay, too. I was amazed by this generosity. I never even had an inkling that she cared. We accepted with great joy.

Strange echoes of our old life remained, a life we seemingly had never lived. In the closet of the apartment we found some clothes we had left behind; Mother's were all too large because she had become very skinny. We went down to the police station and found our little policeman, who was still there, doing the same thing. It was he who had given the French officer our records and gotten us out of prison. We went across the street and found Jean Nocenti, the photographer, who took our picture. He was happy to see me; he thought I had probably been killed. He did not charge us for the pictures; we had no money anyway.

As we left, Mother said she had something to do, somebody to look up. I did not go with her. I saw many American soldiers in the streets. A fellow told me the Americans had selected this area as a resort for U.S. soldiers. They sent 40,000 GIs here every ten days for R&R. The

Tommy Dorsey Orchestra would be giving a free concert in the Place Massena that evening. I was in seventh heaven: a real American dance band on my first day back as a free man! It could not get any better.

My mother finally returned with something stuffed into her purse. We went back to the apartment, and she pulled out a wad of money. I asked how she was able to get such an amount, and she told me she had sold one of her diamond rings. We now had enough money to live on for quite a while. I found out that Mother had carried all her remaining jewelry with her throughout the war. It was always hidden, and only she knew where. My esteem for her went up; I had never expected her to be so smart.

My first priority was the concert that night. I found a pair of secondhand pants and a shirt and changed out of uniform. It felt good to be a civilian again. The concert was tremendous. These sounds were so different from the Nazi oompah! It was a new world. I met a few of my old buddies, and they were pleased to see me alive. Not much seemed to have changed here during the Nazi occupation. Very few really suffered—only the Jews, most of whom were caught and deported. I heard that the French police did most of the arresting.

The next day I went down to the Promenade des Anglais, but something was missing. The Casino de la Jettée—the place where, at age fourteen, I had seen my first naked lady—was no more. I asked around and was told the German army had demolished this beautiful landmark. They claimed it was sticking too far out into the Mediterranean and would be in the way in case of an Allied invasion. What stupidity. They probably had blown it up just to show how superior they were.

I went to the American headquarters and inquired about the possibility of enlisting in the U.S. Army as an interpreter. I figured that if they would accept me, I would be sent to the United States for basic training, be made a U.S. citizen, and come back to Europe and finally to Germany. It was a pretty good scheme, but it did not work. The officer in charge smiled and said I was a dreamer. The army would never send a Partisan guerrilla fighter to Germany; I might kill a lot of Germans just to get even.

The officer suggested that I apply for a job with the U.S. Army in Nice. I did so and to my surprise was hired as a messenger. I drove around town in a Jeep posting bulletins for the soldiers about current shows and entertainment throughout the city. It took about three hours in the morning, and for this I was paid and given a terrific meal in an American mess hall, which was better than the money. I could not buy that much excellent food for all the money in France. It was a lifesaver for me. I began to gain weight again.

One day I happened to pass by the last place we had rented in Nice. I went to see the landlady, a crippled old woman who always sat in the window of her apartment. I wanted to taunt her and her Nazi husband. She was surprisingly friendly to me. We had left a few things behind, and she gave them to me. She told me her husband had been arrested by the liberation army and was eventually shot for treason. I was glad; I had always hated him.

Finally, she told me there was a telegram for us. It had come over a year ago, right after France had been liberated. It was from my sister, Edith, in Cuba, asking about our whereabouts. A paid reply was attached. I ran to the post office and drew up an answer. I realized that by now Edith must have been sure we had not survived. Very gently I explained that Mother and I had made it through the war alive but that we had not heard from

26. In Nice, France, June 1945.

Father. She wired back, overjoyed, and immediately sent a one hundred dollar bill by airmail. That was a lot of money, and worth even more on the black market. Things started to look up.

So far I hadn't thought a lot about what might have happened to Dad. It was hard to know what to think. Although we hadn't heard from him, that didn't mean he hadn't tried to contact us. Communications were very spotty in Eastern Europe, where, presumably, he had been taken. Perhaps he was in a hospital somewhere, or in custody, as Mother and I had been upon our return to France. Anything might have happened, and we weren't going to speculate upon his fate. We simply waited.

But we were not optimistic, especially when word began to filter out about the Nazi atrocities and the death camps. I was stunned at how elaborate the Nazi killing machine had been. According to the reports, millions of people had perished in a very short time. I was unwilling to believe this; it wasn't possible. Then, slowly but surely, death camp survivors started to arrive in Nice. Most came from Auschwitz. None of them wanted to talk at first, but after a few weeks these pathetic-looking people started to tell their tales, and the horror became real: the vastness of the Nazi final solution, the millions dehumanized and slaughtered without remorse. I still wanted to believe Dad was alive and was going to return to us, but it was more and more difficult to remain hopeful.

Then I met Franz Bergner. He was the brother of Elizabeth Bergner, the Hollywood film star. They were originally from Vienna. Franz was always in trouble with the law, and Dad tried to help him, letting him take cuts of material to sell door to door. Dad never asked him for money; Franz always paid whenever he could, and Dad never pushed him.

Franz told me he'd seen Dad in Auschwitz. Franz was a *capo*, a Jewish enforcer enlisted by the Nazis to beat and mistreat inmates. He told me Dad had died shortly before the Nazis evacuated the camp, just before liberation. He said it was just as well, because Dad was so weak he never would have survived the death march out of Auschwitz that the inmates had been forced to make. In tears, he told me he had taken Dad under his wing and had managed to guide him through all of the selections and hoped to get him through alive. Finally, starvation and disease wore him down, and the Nazis had him carried to the crematorium. The flames consumed him while he was still alive.

The pain I felt was almost unbearable. I now knew that Dad was dead and that he had suffered horribly. I never told Mother how Dad had died. In fact, she did not even believe me when I told her

27. In Nice, France, June 1945.

he was dead and was not coming back. I knew she was aware of the existence of the death camps. Her best friend had returned to Nice and told her of the Auschwitz terror. This woman was the only survivor among her family. One SS showed her the smoke coming out of the chimney and told her to pay attention. "Here goes your mother," he said to her as he hit her in the head. Mother had a hard time believing this.

◻ ◊ ◻

The news of Dad's death was our first indication that our lives were not going to get back to normal anytime soon. More bad news followed: I was not going to get a work permit. The authorities explained that the only way to become eligible was to enlist in the French expeditionary forces in Indochina for two years. I would then become a French citizen, and all my problems would be over. I told them to shove it. I had just come out of a war, and I did not cherish the idea of getting into another one.

We went to the American consulate in Nice to inquire about the status of the visas Dad had applied for so long ago. We were told that our papers were missing and had probably been shipped to the nearest consulate, which was in Marseilles. The embassy staff communicated with the consul general and started the ball rolling for us to reapply. Unfortunately, the waiting period was now twenty-one years. We were still on the Polish quota, since Dad had been born in Poland. It apparently would be too difficult to change us to the Austrian quota, where we belonged. I still don't know why.

We refused to give up; Mother started looking around for other options. What else could we do? Meanwhile, I had to try to make some money. I went to see a friend who ran a small bar in a side street in the center of town. He had enlarged his operation and was now also serving food. He said he'd pay me to accost GIs and bring them into the restaurant for steak and fries. I got one hundred francs a head. This went pretty well; the soldiers went crazy over fresh meat. I worked from five to eleven every night and managed to make quite a bit of money. It never occurred to me that there was an acute shortage of meat everywhere; I never asked where the steaks came from. Sometimes I was given a free meal, and it tasted so good! Much later I learned that the steaks were in reality horse meat. I was strongly urged to keep my mouth shut; not wanting to get mutilated, I obeyed.

Another income opportunity soon came my way. Next door to the restaurant was a quaint little whorehouse. The practitioners there said that if I would promote their services and point the well-fed soldiers in their direction, they would give me a percentage of the take. I got a good response; the GIs usually had a lot of money to spend and wanted to have all the fun they could before their ten days of vacation were over. I made many friends among the American soldiers, and I enjoyed them very much. They told me what a wonderful land America was. Everyone hoped to see me there, and I was invited to come to visit when I arrived.

I was managing to make a living, but I realized that if I could corral more soldiers into the restaurant, maybe I could start saving a little money. I talked two of my buddies into buying a very used car, a Renault, and we became partners. We'd drive around looking for customers and give them a free ride to the restaurant and/or the bordello. Our venture went well until the old Renault had had enough. We lost our investment, and I was back to square one. In addition, my job as an army messenger was abolished, and I had to look for new sources of income.

In desperation, I started passing counterfeit money. The French were in the process of changing their currency, and in the meantime they printed temporary bills. Nothing was written on these bills to indicate that counterfeiting was a punishable offense; therefore, people were printing their little hearts out, and I was able to buy these bills at a 50 percent discount. I spent this money in all kinds of stores. The police got to me eventually, but they didn't do anything; just about everybody was passing bad bills. Eventually the franc was devalued, and everybody had to exchange the bills at the post office. Only real money was accepted.

Soon thereafter I ran into an old buddy of mine who owned a small photo store and seemed to be doing well. He offered me a part-time job. Although I did not have a work permit, he was willing to take a chance. He needed me for half of each day to print snapshot orders. I knew how to do this and was even good at it. The job was easy, and I had all afternoon and night to myself. The money was not great, but Edith occasionally sent money. We managed pretty well.

I heard from Uncle Max, my dad's youngest brother. He had survived with the help of a distant relative in Belgium; he now lived in Luxembourg and wanted to see me. I hopped on a train; he picked me up at the station, and we were both thrilled to be reunited. Max was a terrific pianist, and he was making a living playing in a local bar. I was really surprised to hear him play so well. As far as I knew, he had never taken a lesson. Luxembourg had already stopped rationing, and food was plentiful. I enjoyed every meal to the utmost. Max poured it on. Over the weekend his girlfriend came to visit from Belgium. They planned to marry soon, and I was happy for them.

After one week I returned to Nice, loaded up with goodies. I was content for a while, but then I started to get restless again. I was itching to go back to Italy, for some reason; I wanted to see how things had turned out back there. In June I decided to satisfy my curiosity. I took a train from Nice. Shortly after we crossed the border, a bunch of GIs came aboard. They told me it was not necessary to buy train tickets here; the conductors accepted anything that looked like one. I traveled all through northern Italy with a ticket from the Nice tramway.

I went to Cuneo, then to Demonte, and looked up the people I had left behind. The region had fared well; everybody was back to normal, and nobody was particularly excited about my visit. They had no reason to feed or house me now. I went back to Cuneo and stopped to see my two lady friends, the ones who had helped me "desert" from the Italian fascist army, and received a warm welcome. The next day I departed for Torino and went to the headquarters of the Partisan armies. I was entitled to some compensation for my services during the war, and they agreed to pay me. It was a very small amount, but I was pleased.

Upon my return a depressing sense of rootlessness overtook me. There was no future for me in Italy. I had no desire to go back to Vienna, either; there was nobody left there. Everyone had been deported and finally killed in various concentration camps. The Austrian Nazis had done their job well. Their country was now Jewless. And I was now the proverbial wandering Jew.

I looked to America, for which I still had great hopes. I concentrated on improving my English, hanging out with GIs during most of my free time, which I had a lot of now. One American took a liking to me, and I liked him a lot, too. He told me that back in the United States he was Tommy Dorsey's main drummer. I knew he was fibbing, but I still wanted to hear him play. That night I took him to a local club that featured a small jazz combo. He sat in, and I had to admit that he was rather good—maybe not good enough for the Dorsey band, but certainly good enough for me. I loved his company.

The next evening he brought his "girlfriend" along. Most GIs hooked into one girl for their ten-day stay in Nice, paying for the pleasure of one steady date rather than switching around all the time. He introduced me to her, and I was immediately attracted to her. Her name was Paulette, and she was very pretty. She did not look like a whore; she had manners and dressed rather nicely. I was very impressed.

We all had a terrific time for the rest of the stay. When the time came for my buddy to return to his unit, we all went to the station to see him off. Finally, the train left. Paulette and I left together. Without saying a word, we walked to her apartment and went straight to bed, making love like I had never known it before. I had never experienced anything like this. I was aware that Paula was older than I (she was thirty) and that she was a prostitute, but it did not matter to me. I loved her, and she really cared for me. She also wanted somebody who would be nice to her, not just have sex with her for some money.

Paula had lost her husband during the Nazi offensive in France. She had two daughters, ages six and seven, who went to private school. Like so many women during the war, Paula could not find legitimate work and was driven to prostitution. I did not hold it against her. I knew she would eventually stop this way of life if she found a good man to marry her. It was not going to be me, though; I was unemployed, and marriage was an impossibility.

However, Paula filled a great gap in my life. Until we met I had been very lonely. I wanted to meet a girl I could get close to, maybe even get married, settle down, and have a family and a normal life. But I was not a good catch. I was a man without a country, unable to make a decent living and always scrambling for income. I lived in a poorly furnished room and owned nothing. And, by and large, the French detested foreigners. Even the American soldiers who had liberated the country from the Nazis were only tolerated at best. The French hated Germans, and they had not lost their dislike for Jews; so I, a German-speaking Jew, was hardly a popular figure.

Paula and I helped each other put form and meaning back into our lives. The war may have ended, but the heartlessness and cruelty hadn't. All we could do was make the best of it and love each other. Eventually we would have to go our separate ways, but for the time being I was happy and content.

28. Copy of Acte de Disparition retracing my father's deportation route to Auschwitz.

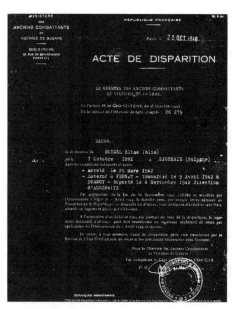

◻ ◇ ◻

News started to come from Vienna. My Aunt Mimi had been deported to Bergen-Belsen and had survived. She wrote of the horror to Mother. She had been assembled with other women in the center of the camp on the final day before liberation. The SS were going to shoot all of them. They opened fire, and Mimi fell to the ground under a lot of bodies but was not hit herself, not even wounded. She lay there motionless for three days and nights, fearing the Nazis would kill her if they found her alive. The Allies finally liberated the camp, found her, nursed her back to health, and sent her back to Vienna. She now lived in a small room in the second district.

Mimi described what had happened to my eighty-six-year-old grandmother Clara. As she was being marched to the trains for deportation to Auschwitz, she fell down in the street. A young soldier from the Wehrmacht approached her as if to help her. Instead, he shot her in the head, and she died instantly. This was probably a blessing; it saved her from enduring any more brutality.

In November 1946 we received a communication from the Ministry of War in Paris. The document outlined in detail my dad's journey from his arrest in Nice to his arrival in Auschwitz, giving all the dates. It indicated that if he did not return within five years of the date of the document, this paper would become his death certificate.

My mother was devastated. Apparently, she had still been waiting for Dad to return, in spite of Franz Bergner's account of his death. Seeing it written on paper seemed to finalize everything for her. I came home that day for lunch and found her lying in bed with blood on her wrists. She had tried to commit suicide. Fortunately, she had no idea how to do it and missed the artery by a mile. I spoke to her at length, and she promised never to do this again.

Mom finally accepted Father's death. To occupy herself she went to the ORT, a Jewish retraining organization, and learned to weave shawls. The finished product was sold in stores. Mother became accomplished at weaving and worked late hours at home to make a little money. This was good therapy for her.

I kept busy, too, joining the Olympic and Gymnastic Club of Nice, an amateur sports organization. The club sponsored a second-division professional soccer team, the Eagles. I spent a lot of time in the clubhouse, played a lot of Ping-Pong, and became pretty good. I also got involved with the soccer team and the players. As a second-division club, it was not very good, but I loved it anyway.

In early 1947 the U.S. military's recreation area in Nice was suddenly abolished. All of the GIs vanished overnight. This was a horrible letdown. Now all connections with the great war were severed. I picked up a camera again and started a little photo business at home. With the help of one hundred dollars from my sister, I was able to purchase all I needed. The largest local photo store, Photo Rey, was willing to use me and gave me some work. I only got paid half the going rate, but at least it was something. To purchase supplies such as papers and chemicals I needed the help of a Frenchman; because I was a foreigner without a permit, neither Kodak nor Lumière could sell to me. So my friend Jeannot did the ordering, and I bought from him. He was very helpful.

I decided to apply for a permit to operate a small business as an artisan. While the application was pending, I was allowed to operate legally. I received permission to photograph at Maxim's, the finest nightclub in Nice. Quite a few American and British officers still came here on furlough. Whenever they were in the company of a lady of the night, they usually wanted a picture, if for no other reason than to show off later. I charged one thousand francs for three 5 x 7 prints delivered the next morning to their hotel.

Around this time, the Nice soccer club went through some important changes. The city, as a world tourist center, was no longer willing to be represented by a second-division club. The municipal government took over the team, purchased a bunch of players from first-division teams, and worked toward winning the league championship and ascending to the first division. The club moved into a brand-new stadium and started to attract national interest.

29. With my mother in Nice, France, May 1946.

I knew the team's new officers, and they gave me a photographer's pass from the International Federation of Football (FIFA). This enabled me to get into any stadium in the country, sit behind the goal line, and take pictures of the games. Armed with this powerful tool, I went to see the editors of *Le Patriote de Nice et du Sud-Est*. This Communist-affiliated publication was the only one of the three local papers that did not have a steady sports photographer. I was given the job, but as usual I was hired off the books for half the going rate because I did not have a work permit. Since I loved the game so much, I thought of the job more as pleasure than as work. Anyway, I only had to work Sundays, and my photographs were published every week with my name underneath for all to see. I was famous yet still not legal.

My photography business began to take off. I got so busy that I took one of my friends in with me as a partner. He managed to get us a contract with a nightclub in Cannes. We were permitted to photograph there three times a week. Every little bit helped. But the extra income only went so far, because the markets were still pretty empty. There was still hunger in

France. Once a week the United States sent a load of flour to help out, and every Sunday we were able to buy white bread in the bakery. The Soviets, not wanting to be outdone, also sent flour. Theirs was unsifted and very dark, almost inedible, but it was received and eaten with gratitude. It amazed me how long it took the country to get back to prewar conditions.

Meanwhile, my relationship with Paulette came to a screeching halt. After the U.S. Army left, she continued to work in assorted whorehouses around town, and we spent very little time together. One day she met a man who was quite a bit older than she. He had a lot of money, and he fell in love with her and wanted to marry her and take care of her two girls. She accepted and moved in with him. I hated to lose her companionship but wished her well. She was very special to me. I never found out where she moved or if they got married. I hope she found happiness.

I was a free man again, and there were plenty of females around. The closing of the U.S. Army's entertainment base left Nice with a glut of prostitutes. Most became dependent on the U.S. Navy for business. Every week large and small ships docked in Villefranche, and thousands of sailors came ashore. Many had been at sea for six months at a time, and all they wanted was women. I knew a lot of prostitutes and ended up running something of a referral service. I was well compensated by both parties for my recommendations. The sailors gave me cigarettes and such; the women paid me with favors only they could give.

The best-looking women were found at Maxim's. These were classy women—well-dressed, educated, and terrific in bed. Some nights were not as good as others. If by four in the morning they had not connected with anybody, I could usually take them home for a cup of coffee. Sometimes they asked me to take pictures of their babies. Most had children fathered by American soldiers, and they took very good care of them. I would take the assignment and receive payment in American cigarettes. On the black market, they brought a pretty penny. But in spite of the abundance of women surrounding me, I never found another Paulette.

□ ◊ □

In 1947, the Nice soccer club finally won the championship of the second division and was promoted to the national division. The city, committed to fielding a winning team, acquired some more good players, and anticipation rose for the upcoming season. The city rallied around their new heroes, and I was right in the middle of everything. I was now a top sports photographer, and everybody knew me.

Everything seemed to be going great when the bomb fell: I received notification that my application to become an artisan had been rejected. I was forbidden by law to continue to operate my business. What a blow! I took all my equipment out of the apartment and moved it into my partner's basement, and we continued to operate illegally. Nobody cared. The police either were very lax or did not know about the rejection of my application. My photos still appeared every week with my name under them, and nobody paid attention.

At least, not for a while. Then a rival photographer who wanted my job at the paper filed a complaint. I was called to the police station. The detective who had my file started the conversation with, "So, you are a photographer?" I was in trouble, and I knew it. But I'd talked myself out of worse pinches than this one. Nonchalantly, I answered, "As I told the chief of police yesterday after I returned with his daughter from our date. . . ." Before I could finish the sentence, my interrogator interrupted me. He said he was unaware that I knew the chief; he apologized and tore up the file. I was free to go. My gambit was not entirely a lie: I *did* know the chief's daughter, but the chief didn't want me to bother her because he didn't think I was good enough for her.

Anyway, I was still in business. The *Patriote* applied for a work permit for me so I could do business legally. It took them exactly ten minutes to obtain it. What a farce.

A new sports paper was preparing for publication, and a friend's father was running the show. The paper was printed on Monday mornings and covered all the sports news from around the country. It was a great idea. I was asked to take photographs at local sporting events. The *Patriote* gave me permission to work for the new periodical but reserved the right to have the first pick of my photos, which was fair. The new paper was called *Sport Lundi*, Sports Monday. It had no money yet, so everybody worked for free. I even had to deliver papers to the newsstands early every Monday morning. For this purpose the paper gave me a 1924 Peugeot Camionette, a tiny truck with only one door and four bald tires. I was to keep it and use it for myself when I was not delivering papers. Now I was in business; I was motorized. The truck ran surprisingly well most of the time. Once in a while it needed a push, which I could always get.

Through the *Patriote* I was able to sell photographs to a sports magazine in Paris. Every week I shipped two or three pictures by train, which supplemented my income nicely.

The sports paper did really well; nobody made any money, but everybody pushed hard.

In the summer of 1948 both papers asked me to go to Florence, Italy, to cover an international soccer game between France and Yugoslavia. It was the rubber match, and the winner would qualify for the World Cup. I was very happy to be chosen. Two players from the Nice soccer club were selected to play for the French side, so there was great interest in our region.

I left Nice in the company of a bunch of fanatical supporters. After our arrival in Florence I checked into our hotel and immediately went into town. The beauty of this city was overwhelming. The sidewalks were inlaid mosaic, and the church domes and monuments were golden. I could not get enough. I took it all in and was grateful to my parents for having exposed me to culture while we still lived amidst it.

The next day was game day, and I had much to do. I made arrangements with the conductor of the train to send my film to Nice. First I sent one roll as an exposure test; the real thing would follow after the game. It would arrive in Nice before me and just make the Monday paper. Jeannot would pick up the films and do the developing and printing as a favor to me.

30. In Monte Carlo, summer 1947.

The test roll went well; now it was show-time. I went to the stadium early, got my place on the goal line, and waited for the action to begin. The game was good. It was tied at one until late in the second half. With the clock winding down, Luciano, one of the Nice players, got the ball about forty meters from the goal and let go. He just wanted to bring the ball in front of the Yugoslav net. To the surprise of everyone, especially Luciano himself, the ball sailed into the goal, and France won the game. Everybody was speechless but elated. And I was happier than anyone—I had caught it all on film.

I ran to the train station as fast as I could, caught the express to Nice, and sent my film on ahead. All I could do now was hope for the best. I had no idea whether the film would be delivered on time or whether the negatives would be developed and printed in time for the Monday morning editions. I had learned a long time ago that you can't always rely on other people.

Our train left late that night. I was anxious to see the paper when I arrived. We reached Nice at about eleven in the morning, and I immediately picked up a copy of *Sport Lundi* at the station. I didn't even mind paying for it. I looked at the front page and saw one of my shots of the winning goal. It almost covered the whole page! I had never seen a picture that large in any newspaper. I opened the centerfold and found my photos all over the double page. My name was everywhere.

In the afternoon the *Patriote* came out, filled with nothing but my pictures. Just about everything I shot had been published. Everybody congratulated me at length. I was very proud.

31. With newspaper crew covering the Tour de France.

My career prospects seemed bright. I was still working at Maxim's and at the club in Cannes. The latter was a very special place. Its floor show always featured transvestites. These fellows looked better than many women I had known. They were star material. Once in a while one of them would ask me to dance. Everybody was always jealous of me, wondering how I could attract such beautiful women. I got a charge out of it. These guys were great dancers, and they got me a lot of business. I did publicity shots of the stars of the show, got paid well, and never received any complaints. Once or twice someone would make a pass at me. I'd politely decline and leave it at that, which satisfied everybody. I had no problem with these performers, who seemed to be gentle, kind people.

Nice hosted a lot of festivals, including an international jazz festival, where I had the good fortune to meet Louis Armstrong. He was an exceptional person, and his group was fabulous. Every night after their scheduled performance they'd go jamming in local clubs, and I'd go with them. It was the experience of a lifetime.

Satchmo spoke freely about the United States' racial problems, which I had been unaware of. He said the camaraderie he and I were able to enjoy in France would not have been possible back home. White people adored him while he was on stage, but after the show he and all the black performers would usually go back to Harlem. They were not welcome in white establishments.

I could not understand this sort of discrimination. Hadn't the United States just fought the Nazis and liberated Europe from the worst perpetrators of racial discrimination the world has ever known? Armstrong had a lot of understanding and showed a lot of feeling when I talked about the Jews' dilemma during the Hitler years. He, too, was Jewish; his ancestors had been enslaved by Jewish people, and slaves usually took their master's religion. This poor man was black and Jewish? Maybe I didn't have it so rough.

Maxim's hired a new band—Willy Sansky and his Salon Orchestra—and I befriended the musicians. Willy, his brother, and his dad, the main members of the group, were Polish Jews. I had no idea how they had survived the Holocaust, nor did I ever ask. Willy and I hit it off rather well. His girlfriend, Manoutrel, was the singer in the band. She was very attractive; she always appeared in a sarong and wore lots of flowers in her hair. Her sister Lanatrel was also in show business. She was a Hawaiian hula dancer and stood over six feet tall.

Willy had to play in San Remo one weekend and asked me if I cared to come along. Naturally, I went. Our first night at dinner we all ordered steak. When the meal came, the steaks looked gray. We sent them back and told the waiter we wanted them cooked medium rare. They returned, medium rare—but still gray. After a lengthy conversation with the waiter and the cook, we got to the bottom of the problem. Italy still did not have any beef. They had to breed new cattle herds to replace what the Germans had destroyed. Only veal was available; that's what we were eating. The cook took the meat back and cooked it to perfection, and we ate a very tasty veal dinner.

My sports photography kept me busy, and my business started to expand a little. With my contacts from the newspaper I was even able to photograph at the casino in Monte Carlo. The event was the introduction of a new game: craps, brought over from America, was to be played here for the first time. Photography was not allowed in the gambling area, but I managed to smuggle a small camera into the room and was able to take one shot without being detected. The photograph was published in a top Parisian newspaper. I was paid well and received national recognition.

By now France was emerging from the misery the Germans had created. Food was ample again, and rationing had been terminated. I could not believe the riches in all the stores. All one needed was money, which Mother and I still did not

have. I was twenty-five years old now
and ready for some stability, but my
future was totally up in the air. I still
couldn't become a French citizen
unless I spent two years in the army,

*32. With singer Manoutrel
and bandleader Willy
Sansky in Juan les Pins,
France, April 1949.*

which I refused to do. My application for a U.S. visa remained
on hold. I was even debating whether Mother and I should
return to Vienna and try to resume our lives. But anti-Semitism
had not subsided there, and I was not about to put myself back
in the path of that evil current.

At about this time I received a letter from Edith. It was
postmarked from New York! She had received her immigration
visa and, because of the difficult political conditions in Cuba,
had moved to the United States. Fritzi Weiss had opened a
bridge club in Manhattan, and Edith worked for her as a wait-
ress, serving dinner to the players. All the patrons were immigrants from Vienna, and therefore there was no language barrier.

Her husband, Duno, had gone to Mexico and initiated
divorce proceedings. I was still looking for a way to get back at

him for his betrayal of our family. Had he not purchased Cuban visas for his impresario instead of for us, we could have made it safely to Cuba before the war began. As far as I was concerned, Duno was personally responsible for my father's death. I had never hated anybody as I hated this man. It pleased me that he was severed from our family and that I would never have to lay eyes on him again.

My mother was determined to get to New York so we could be reunited with Edith. She was in touch with all the Jewish organizations in the country. The Hebrew Immigration Aid Society (HIAS) became interested in our case. My dad had been a very big contributor to their cause. Nobody at that organization could understand why we were unable to emigrate to the United States. We had been classified as displaced persons, but we had never been deported or placed in a Nazi camp. That seemed to be the difference. The HIAS promised to continue working in our behalf and to notify us as soon as an answer could be found.

◻ ◇ ◻

My last trip with the soccer club was to Strasbourg. The club had hired a biplane, and there was one vacancy; when the seat was offered to me, I was happy to take it. We arrived the evening before the game and were driven to a hostel. Dinner was extraordinary, very German—sausage, sauerkraut, potatoes, and lots of beer. The next morning a few players and I went across the border into Germany. Cologne was still under French occupation. It was delightful to see Germans getting some of their own medicine. The French were not very kind to them, and I loved it.

The game was played, and our club lost. We boarded the plane and took off. After a minute or so, the pilot turned back; it seemed that a small problem in one of the two engines had to be repaired. We were stuck there for another night. I called the paper in Nice and told them as much as possible about the game and its highlights.

We finally made it back home the next day. That afternoon I went to the *Patriote*'s sports department to check in. Everybody acted strangely, and I did not know what was going on. Finally, the head reporter showed me the evening edition, which had not hit the stands yet. On the sports page, the top article was about the Strasbourg game. Under the headline, to my amazement, I read: "By our special envoy, Henri Burger." The article was almost word for word what I had telephoned the night before. It must have been better than what came off the wire. I was really pleased. I had seen my name in the paper many times before, but never as a writer.

After everybody had congratulated me on my writing prowess and the backslapping finally ended, I realized this was not such a great honor. I did not get paid for the article, and one could not buy food with glory alone. This incident put my future in France into depressing perspective. The law did not accept me as an equal; I was still a foreigner and thus could be exploited with impunity. I was now and would always remain a refugee. I was more desperate than ever to leave France.

Yet it seemed it would take a miracle. I placed all my hopes on the HIAS. I had learned that the United States now allowed many displaced persons still in Germany to immigrate. Quotas were being bypassed, and whole families were being shipped to various American cities. Most were concentration camp survivors languishing in displaced-person settlements throughout Germany and Austria. Understandably, these people were first in line, because they had nowhere to go. But I had nowhere to go, either; though I was in beautiful Nice, the place everybody wanted to be, I was languishing nonetheless.

It could be worse, I realized. I could be back in Vienna, where Jews still couldn't get jobs and where *saujude* and other assorted names were still deeply embedded in the vocabulary. I had heard that the Austrians were quite happy with Hitler's final solution. Very few Jews had returned to Vienna, and they were made unwelcome and left as fast as they came.

My own circumstances were far better. Yet I couldn't help feeling that I had somehow ended up back in a forced residence, physically safe but politically, economically, and spiritually oppressed. I wanted more out of life than a work permit and a subsistence wage; after the dangers I'd faced and the battles I'd fought, I deserved real opportunity, real freedom. I wondered if I would ever get it.

7

Going Home

Like a bolt of lightning, it came from out of nowhere. A telegram from the U.S. consulate in Marseilles informed us that our original visa application papers had been found in the basement during a routine check. Our quota number was up, and if we came to Marseilles for a physical examination we would be eligible for U.S. immigration visas. I cannot describe my feelings and thoughts at that time; overwhelmed, I read the telegram over and over again.

Mother went to the HIAS representative in Nice to ask what to do now. The guidance was excellent. First, we had to get a valid passport; we were still carrying our old brown Nazi documents emblazoned with the red "J." The HIAS made arrangements with the Austrian embassy in Paris, and we were issued new passports. The next thing I knew, Mom and I were on our way to Marseilles. It was a nice drive, but my mother did not enjoy it. She just wanted to get this process over with; she spoke no French—just a few words mixed with hand signals— so she had to rely entirely on me. The French were still not prone to offering a helping hand to foreigners.

I did not know my way around Marseilles, but I managed to get us to the clinic for our examinations. I was scared to death. I had slept with so many loose women since the end of the war that I was sure I had some kind of venereal disease. I said nothing to my mother. If my sleeping with prostitutes had caused me to fail the physical, she probably would have said it served me right. I had no idea which diseases would disqualify me for entry to the United States. After an agonizing wait, I went into the examining room. The doctor looked me over, and a nurse took a blood sample. I crossed my fingers and hoped for the best.

A short time later we were on our way to the U.S. consulate. The consul received us in person. He made a long apology about the mislaid documents and said angrily that we could have been in the United States a long time ago had it not been for that error. Then he had us rise and raise our right hands and swear to be faithful to the Constitution of the United States of America. I could do that with ease; America was the only country that wanted us. The word *Jew* was never mentioned in any of the papers we saw and signed. The consul wished us much luck in our new country. He said that as soon as our passports arrived from the Austrian embassy in Paris, the visas would be entered and forwarded to us in Nice.

It was all so easy and fast that I had to pinch myself. Mother was unmoved, as usual. Only one hurdle remained: I had to go back to the doctor's office to get the results of my blood test. To my everlasting relief, I was told that my sample was clean and that I was very healthy. I could breathe again! I never told Mom of the distress I had gone through. I had been very lucky, because the odds were against me; in France, venereal diseases were so common they were thought of as childhood diseases.

On November 25, 1949, our passports were executed and shipped to Marseilles. Our U.S. immigration visas were stamped into them on December 1. The HIAS made all our travel arrangements for us. Passage was booked on the luxury liner *Ile de France* because Mother refused to fly on an American transport plane. It would have been a bumpy flight, and she had heard that the planes were not safe. The fact that they had safely transported millions of Allied troops and large amounts of equipment meant nothing to her.

Before leaving, we had to put various affairs in order. First, to get a French exit visa we had to clear the tax slate. That was easy; Mother and I had never legally worked and therefore had no official income. Nevertheless, we had to go to the tax office to get a release. As we stood waiting, I found out that nobody paid taxes in France. All it took was a little envelope with some cash, which the agent pocketed. The bill was stamped "paid," and that was it. No wonder the country was in such bad shape. Next we had to get permission to export American money. Everybody was allowed to take the nominal sum of ten dollars out of the country. This amount had to be entered into the passport. I suppose there must have been other ways to take money to a foreign country, but I never tried to find out. I was just happy to be going to America at last.

The HIAS furnished train tickets to Paris. From there we would go by train to Le Havre, arriving January 4. Edith was so happy to hear the good news. We had not seen each other since 1940. I told Mother to quit selling her jewelry, because we did not need any money that we could not take with us. The *Patriote* owed me quite a bit of money, and I was able to collect. We were doing fine, enjoying good times for a change. I went to Maxim's every night and just relaxed. By chance I met a young lady, probably the only Jewish hooker in the southeast of France, and we fell in together. I never asked her how she survived the Nazis and the war. It was just good to be with a Jew. The French had done a superb job for the Nazis; there were almost no Jews left in the southeast of France. The woman's name was Helene; she was a very warm human being, the first Jewish woman I had ever slept with.

At the time I never thought I might eventually miss all this. After all, Nice was a wonderful place to live. Tourists from all over the world came here to vacation, and I was going to leave it all. But this was a small price to pay for freedom and liberty.

□ ◊ □

As the time of our departure came nearer and nearer, I started to get mentally ready. I really did not own anything: just one white suit, two shirts, some underwear and socks, and a camera. My baggage was going to be very light. Mother did not own much more than I. But since we had left Vienna, possessions had meant very little. Our priorities had somehow shifted.

For the first time, I started to think about what had happened to us, and rage swelled within me. Many of our family members had died at the hands of Nazis. Although I did not know those from Poland and Hungary personally, I knew of them. I could never find anything out about my grandfather. Even Aunt Mimi could not get any information on how he died. I hoped it was of old age.

I also began to recognize how painful our years in France had been. When we had come to this country in 1940 as political refugees, we had been classified as tourists. Nobody was allowed to make a living; everybody had to be self-sufficient. Ten years later, not much had changed. The few remaining survivors of the Holocaust were still classified as tourists and held at arm's length by the French people. We had not been murdered or openly discriminated against here, but clearly we were not wanted. So as we boarded the train to Paris and left the south of France forever, I felt no regrets, only relief.

Upon our arrival in Paris, we were met by representatives from the HIAS. It was incredible how well organized this agency was. They handed us coupons for a hotel, vouchers for a restaurant nearby, and Metro tickets. However, Mother had made arrangements for us to stay with the Wald family, old friends of hers from Vienna. We went home with them, enjoyed the wonderful meal they had prepared, and reminisced about Vienna. Wald and his son had work permits, and they intended to stay in France for the time being. They were not as angry at the French as I was. They had managed to survive the war in a small town near Paris, and the French family that hid them was good to them. We all agreed on one thing: we would never return to Vienna.

Mother and I had a good night's sleep, and the next morning we went to the HIAS office. All our paperwork was ready. The *Ile de France* was sailing from Le Havre the next day at noon. On the morning of January 4, 1950, we boarded the train to Le Havre. It was only a few hours' ride, and we were in the company of a few dozen other Jewish immigrants. Everybody was full of joy and hope.

33. Just before my departure for the United States.

But after about one hour, the train stopped abruptly. It moved back a little, then forward again. This went on for about half an hour. Rumors flew: the French authorities were going to take our last few belongings; our visas had been cancelled; we were being deported to our nations of origin. To European Jews in the aftermath of the Holocaust, anything seemed possible. Finally, the train reversed course and headed back to Paris. An official of the HIAS who was traveling with us announced that the crew of the *Ile de France* had gone on strike. The boat was not going anywhere. And neither were we. To the bitter end, freedom remained an elusive goal.

Back we went to the Walds'. I don't think they were really happy to have us back. We did not know how long this was going to take, but we found out the next morning. We had been booked on a new ship, the SS *Vendam*, which was to depart from Rotterdam on January 20.

I was disappointed but intended to make the best of the situation. I recalled that a Parisian sports magazine owed me for four pictures. I went to the office, and a reporter named Jules came to take me inside. He gave me my money immediately, and as I was about to leave he invited me to have dinner with his family that evening. I accepted. I had a wonderful time with my new friends, and Jules invited me to a first-division soccer game the next Sunday at the Park des Princes, a magnificent stadium in the Bois de Boulogne. I was excited. It was almost like being back in Vienna when Dad took me to our Sunday soccer games.

The next few days were frantically busy. I had to schlepp Mother to the Dutch and Belgium consulates to obtain transit visas so we could travel through both countries. Our desire to get out of Europe was acute, and it was mixed with an undercurrent of anxiety, a fear that something would go wrong, that we would once again be denied, that our nightmare would never end.

On January 19 we were met by an HIAS representative at the train station. He and one other man took the trip with us. Now the group was down to only about a dozen or so Jewish immigrants. We left in the afternoon and crossed into Belgium that evening. We were not allowed to leave the train on any of the stops, because we had only transit visas. The next morning we entered Holland. As I looked out the window, my eyes were met by piles of rubble and debris such as I had never before seen. The entire city had been destroyed. I was told the Nazis had bombed Rotterdam three days after the Dutch had surrendered. That was typical.

Two limousines met us at the train station and took us to what appeared to be the port of Rotterdam. The SS *Vendam* was waiting for us, ready to sail. We were rushed onto the ramp and got on deck. No sooner was I aboard than the ship went into motion. It was that fast; I could not even say thank you to the HIAS folks who had gotten us here. I was sailing to America!

□ ◊ □

A steward grabbed my baggage, as small as it was, and led me to a cabin down under. I shared the space with three other passengers. Two were Chassidic Jews on their way to Chicago. The smell of garlic in this cabin was incredible. They had brought their own food to make sure they kept kosher. They intended to live on salami, and they had brought a lot of it. Mother was housed in a different section, in a cabin with three camp survivors. She was thrilled, because everybody spoke her language.

Our trip was to last twelve days or so, with stops in England and Bermuda. This time of the year the sea was rough, to say the least. As I went to the dining room for breakfast one day, I suddenly got very ill and vomited all over the beautiful wooden wall before me. Mother was similarly distressed and never appeared in the dining room after the first day of the voyage.

In some cabins next to mine were a bunch of German citizens emigrating to the promised land. To my horror, I figured out that they were all former SS officers! How could this be? Why were they going my way, and what were they going to do once we were all in America? All I could hear coming out of their mouths was arrogance. They acted as if nothing had happened, as if they had won the war and the Third Reich still existed.

One of the young Americans onboard tried to help put me at ease. He said I had to get over the war. What had happened was in the past. He tried to compare it to a sharp knife. When you first get a knife, it is very sharp and cuts really well. With time, the edge becomes duller and duller. Finally, it can't cut anymore and you put it away. He said my pain was like a knife blade; it would become duller and duller as time went by, until it couldn't cut me anymore. You don't understand, I told him. I don't want to forget this pain; I don't want to just put it away. I want it to remain sharp and crystal clear. I'll remember what the Nazis did until hell freezes over.

I did try to forget the Nazis onboard, but it was very difficult. My Chassidic friends were a constant target of these SS men, but they totally ignored the abuse. All they were concerned with was how they could get their salami into America. They had heard customs might confiscate food. I assured them that in America plenty of kosher food was available, which calmed them down. Meanwhile, I found out that the Germans already had jobs in the United States. They were brought over to work for some government-connected agency, although I never found out which one.

□ ◊ □

On February 7, 1950, the ship slowed down. The skies cleared, and the sun came out. Slowly, we sailed past the Statue of Liberty, and a very warm feeling came over me. This was what I had been dreaming about for more than ten years. My American friend stood next to me and put his arm around my shoulder. He was very happy for me. I took my first look at New York harbor, with the skyscrapers rising so far overhead. It was a sight never to be forgotten. I was a happy man. The ship swung left and was picked up by a tug, and we docked in Hoboken, New Jersey. I was in America.

I looked over the railing and spotted my sister, Edith, waving at us. She was standing there in the cold with a distant cousin of ours, cousin Francis. I had heard of her; her parents had come to the United States after World War I.

The customs officers came aboard and set up shop. One by one, we came before them. Our visas were checked carefully, and our quota number was confirmed. One more stamp in the passport and it was all over. The officers were happily surprised that I could speak English; very few newcomers were able to do so. Very gently, they told me that I was now in

34. Harry Burger today.

the United States and that I was welcome here. They explained that in five years I could apply for U.S. citizenship and that I would love becoming an American. I said, "You don't know how much."

I knew what it meant to be a persecuted minority, what it meant to be a prisoner, what it meant to be a soldier, what it meant to be a refugee. Now, at last, I would know what it meant to be truly free. Mother was ahead of me as we came down the ramp. My body was erect, and my head was straight on my shoulders. When my left foot touched the ground, I knew I had come home. This was the beginning.

Epilogue

First, they came for the Jews, and I did not speak out because I was not a Jew.

Then they came for the Communists, and I did not speak out because I was not a Communist.

Then they came for the trade unionists, and I did not speak out because I was not a trade unionist.

Then they came for me, and there was no one left to speak out for me.

—Pastor Martin Niemoller
Encyclopedia of the Holocaust, Vol. 3
Macmillan Publishing Co.

Afrikacorps. Rommel's elite fighting forces in North Africa.

Allies. Nations fighting Nazi Germany during World War II, namely the United States, Great Britain, and the Soviet Union.

Anschluss. Annexation of Austria by Germany on March 13, 1938.

Anti-Semitism. Prejudice against Jews. The word was first coined by nineteenth- and twentieth-century racists, who used it to add racial dimensions to already existing religious and socioeconomic prejudicial views.

Aryan race. Term applied by the Nazis to people of northern European extraction. Their aim was to avoid the "bastardization" of the German "race" and to preserve the purity of European blood.

Auschwitz. Death camp in upper Silesia, Poland, thirty-seven miles west of Krakow. Two million people were executed between 1942 and 1944. As many as twenty-four thousand victims were put to death every day.

Axis. The Axis powers originally included Nazi Germany, Italy, and Japan. They were later joined by Bulgaria, Croatia, Hungary, and Slovakia.

Bergen-Belsen. Nazi concentration camp where thousands of inmates died of starvation and disease.

Boycott. Shortly after taking control of Germany, the Nazis declared a nationwide boycott of Jewish-owned businesses. This was done to demonstrate their might and ideological purpose.

Buchenwald. One of three original concentration camps, opened in 1933. Located in central Germany. Thousands of Jews were eventually imprisoned and later executed.

Concentration camps. A group of labor and prison camps for all "enemies" of the Nazi regime (e.g., communists, socialists, monarchists, gypsies, homosexuals, and other "antisocials"). In 1938 Jews were added to the list simply because they were Jews.

Crystal Night (Kristallnacht). "Night of the broken glass." Name for the violent pogroms, or terror attacks, carried out against the Jews in Germany and Austria November 9–10, 1938.

Dachau. Concentration camp located near Munich in southwestern Germany. Opened in 1933.

Deportation. The "resettlement" of Jews from Nazi-occupied territories to labor or death camps.

Displaced person (DP). A refugee from his or her country in flight from terror and oppression. After the Holocaust, DP camps were set up throughout Europe as temporary detention camps for many of those liberated from Nazi concentration camps.

Eichmann, Adolf (1906–1962). SS lieutenant colonel and head of the "Jewish Section" of the Gestapo. He was instrumental in implementing the Final Solution. On May 11, 1960, he was arrested by members of the Israeli Secret Service and was smuggled from Argentina to Israel. Eichmann was tried in Jerusalem, convicted, and sentenced to death. He was executed on May 11, 1962.

Final Solution. The Nazi term for the plan to destroy the Jews of Europe—the "Final Solution of the Jewish Question." The program was deceptively disguised as "resettlement to the East."

Gestapo. German contraction for Geheime Staatspolizei (Secret State Police).

Ghetto. A medieval system, revived by the Nazis, designating an area in a city where Jews were restricted and forbidden to leave on penalty of death. They were crowded into a small area with little food and no hygienic facilities. After all inhabitants were deported to death or labor camps, ghettos were destroyed.

Goering, Hermann (1893–1946). When Hitler came to power in 1933, he became air minister of Germany and prime minister of Prussia. In 1939, he became Hitler's successor. He was the head of the Luftwaffe, the German Air Force. Convicted in Nuremberg in 1946, he committed suicide by taking poison two hours before his scheduled execution.

Greater German Reich. Name for an expanded Germany that was intended to include all German-speaking people. It was one of Hitler's most coveted aims.

Grynszpan, Herschel (1921–1943?). A Polish Jewish youth who had emigrated to Paris. Upset over the fate of his parents, who were deported to the Polish border, he shot and mortally wounded Third Secretary Ernst vom Rath on November 7, 1938. This incident was the Nazi excuse for Kristallnacht.

Hitler, Adolf (1889–1945). Führer (leader) and chancellor of the Third Reich from 1933 until his death in 1945.

Hitlerjugend. Military organization for young German boys. The troop was used to instill Nazi values and prepare members for future military service. They were introduced to the front lines before the end of World War II.

Holocaust. The destruction of approximately 6 million Jews by the Nazis between 1933 and 1945.

Kapo. A prisoner in charge of a group of inmates in a concentration camp. These men had usually been criminals before their arrest by the Nazis.

Master race. Term used to designate Germans as a "superior" race.

Mein Kampf. Autobiographical book (My Struggle) written by Hitler during his incarceration in the Landsberg fortress after the Beer-Hall Putch in 1923.

Mussolini, Benito (1883-1945). Fascist dictator of Italy, 1922–1943.

Nazi Party. Short for National Socialist German Workers Party.

Nuremberg Laws. Two anti-Jewish statutes enacted in September 1935 during the Nazi Party's national convention in Nuremberg. The first deprived German Jews of their citizenship and all rights pertinent thereto. The second, the Law for the Protection of German Blood and Honor, outlawed marriages of Jews and non-Jews, forbade Jews from employing German females of childbearing age, and prohibited Jews from displaying the German flag. The Nuremberg Laws carefully established definitions of Jewishness based on bloodlines.

Partisans. Irregular troops engaged in guerrilla warfare, often behind enemy lines. During World War II, this name was given to resistance fighters in Nazi-occupied territories.

SA. Abbreviation for Sturmabteilung, the storm troops of the early Nazi Party.

Selection. The process of choosing victims for the gas chambers in the Nazi camps by separating them from those considered fit to work.

SS. Abbreviation, usually written with two lightning symbols, for Schutzstaffeln (Defense Protective Units). Originally organized as Hitler's personal bodyguards, the SS was transformed into a giant organization by Heinrich Himmler. Many SS units were assigned to the battlefields (Waffen SS). The organization is best known for carrying out the destruction of European Jewry.

Der Sturmer **(The Assailant).** An anti-Semitic German weekly founded and edited by Julius Streicher and published in Nuremberg between 1923 and 1945.

Swastika. *Hackenkreutz* in German. An official symbol of the Nazis to denote Aryan superiority.

Third Reich (Third Empire). The official name for Hitler's regime, which ruled Germany from 1933 to 1945. It was supposed to last for one thousand years.

Volkssturm. Germans sixty years and over drafted into the Wehrmacht toward the end of the war.

Wehrmacht. The German Armed Forces.

INDEX